So You Want to Be a Professor?

This book is dedicated to
Professor George Dinsmore,
who, in 1961 in the Lehigh University Student Union,
while we were eating chocolate fudge sundaes,
suggested that I might make a pretty fair university professor.

P. Aarne Vesilind

So You Want to Be a Professor?

A Handbook for Graduate Students

Sage Publications, Inc.
International Educational and Professional Publisher
Thousand Oaks ■ London ■ New Delhi

For information:

Sage Publications, Inc.
2455 Teller Road
Thousand Oaks, California 91320
E-mail: order@sagepub.com

Sage Publications Ltd.
6 Bonhill Street
London EC2A 4PU
United Kingdom

Sage Publications India Pvt. Ltd.
M-32 Market
Greater Kailash I
New Delhi 110 048 India

Printed in the United States of America

Library of Congress Cataloging-in-Publication Data

Vesilind, P. Aarne.
    So you want to be a professor?: A handbook for graduate students /
by P. Aarne Vesilind.
        p. cm.
    Includes bibliographical references and index.
    ISBN 0-7619-1896-5 (cloth: alk. paper)
    ISBN 0-7619-1897-3 (pbk.: alk paper)
        1. College teaching—Vocational guidance—United States Handbooks,
manuals, etc. 2. College teachers—Employment—United States Handbooks,
manuals, etc. 3. Graduate students—Employment—United States
Handbooks, manuals, etc. I. Title.
        LB1778.2 .V47 2000
        378.1'2—dc21   99-6725

99   00   01   02   03   10   9   8   7   6   5   4   3   2   1

Acquiring Editor:	Harry Briggs
Editorial Assistant:	MaryAnn Vail
Editorial Assistant:	Cindy Bear
Typesetter/Designer:	Marion Warren
Indexer:	Paul Corrington
Cover Designer:	Michelle Lee

Contents

Preface

You probably started observing teachers in secondary school. You knew who the good teachers were, and you could tell what made them good. You also knew that some teachers, no matter how hard they tried, could not teach. Some teachers were bored and boring, and you resented having to sit in their classroom. You just *knew* you could, given the chance, do a better job of teaching.

Paralleling this development was your deepening commitment to your discipline. Undergraduate school was interesting, and going to graduate school seemed like a good idea, mostly because you could spend more time taking the courses you really liked. You continued to develop your skills and now find yourself the "world expert" in your research or scholarly area.

But graduation looms. Decision time. What to do when you grow up?

You would like to combine the two loves of your life—teaching and scholarship—and perhaps build a satisfying and profitable academic career, but you are not sure if this is really what you want or how to go about it if you did decide to seek such employment.

Read on!

This book is written for you. It is intended primarily for senior graduate students who are seriously considering a job in academia.

The book begins with a discussion of available jobs in academia and how to get one. The next chapters cover the teaching part of the job, with some learning theory and discussion on organizing a course, tips on lecturing, and a discussion of alternative teaching techniques. A special chapter is reserved for meeting your first class—a special time for all of us. The next two chapters cover testing and evaluation and advising students. Next are some aspects of research and scholarship and the publication of scholarly material. All this should result in tenure, and the actual procedure for getting tenure is discussed. Chapters 12 and 13 relate to the professor's ethical responsibilities, first to maintain academic integrity in the university system, and second on how not to get fired from a tenured job. Chapter 14 provides information on managing your academic career with a minimum of stress.

Except for the first two chapters on academic employment, the rest of the book would be useful for junior faculty as well, providing them with practical assistance in teaching, research, and publishing.

This book began as a series of class notes for a course I have taught for some years at Duke University to senior engineering graduate students. The enthusiasm and dedication of this small band of future university faculty was the main impetus for collecting our discussions in this text.

I gratefully acknowledge the assistance of many who have read the manuscript and provided comments and suggestions, particularly Christopher Endy, Wendy Gentleman, Drew Endy, James Corbett, Sara Wilson, Lauren Sieg, Julie Rogers, DeeAnne Goodenough-Lashua, and Elizabeth Vesilind.

CHAPTER 1

Employment Opportunities in Academia

Let me be right up front with it. I believe in the basic goodness of the American higher educational system and would recommend a career in the professorate to anyone. But this book is not a propaganda piece for recruiting new professors. Instead, I try to describe the good as well as the ugly aspects of an academic career, and hope that you, the reader, will gain a deeper understanding of the career you are considering. I begin by describing the American educational system, and then discussing the employment opportunities within that system.

The American Higher Educational System

Chaos best describes the American university system. There is no such thing as a "typical American college" or "typical American university." Each of the more than 3,700 institutions of higher learning is unique and employment opportunities for potential faculty vary widely. For our purposes, however, the 3,700 institutions can be categorized to illustrate the diversity and to provide some guidance on what types of academic positions might be available at such institutions. As a potential faculty member, an understanding of this order-out-of-chaos is important because the expectations of you as a faculty member will differ markedly from institution to institution.

The American university has its roots in colleges where the primary purpose was to educate Christian gentlemen, with Harvard being the first. The model adopted resembled that of the English university with emphasis on the classics and a liberal education. A most important event in American university development was the establishment of The Johns Hopkins University in 1876, the first university to offer graduate education based on the German university model. Eventually all large universities incorporated both the English and the German educational systems, emphasizing their responsibilities for educating their students as well as conducting cutting-edge research. Some smaller institutions resisted the German model and remained mostly teaching colleges.

Colleges and universities have diverse historical roots and modern functions and are therefore almost impossible to categorize. The Carnegie Foundation for the Advancement of Teaching has proposed one classification that it finds useful, based mainly on size and Ph.D. production.[1] Their classification is as follows:

Research universities I offer a full range of baccalaureate programs, are committed to graduate education through the doctorate, and give high priority to research. They award 50 or more doctoral degrees each year. In addition, they receive annually $40 million or more in federal support. Examples include Harvard University, UCLA, Case Western Reserve University, University of Illinois, Stanford University, and Cornell University.

Research universities II meet all the criteria for research I institutions except that their annual federal support ranges between $15.5 million and $40 million. Examples include Lehigh University, Oklahoma State University, the University of Delaware, Notre Dame, and the University of Vermont.

Doctoral universities I offer a full range of baccalaureate degrees and have a commitment to graduate education through the doctorate. They award at least 40 doctoral degrees annually in five or more disciplines. Examples are William and Mary, Marquette, Southern Methodist, and Western Michigan.

Doctoral universities II meet all the criteria for Doctoral I institutions except that they award annually at least 10 doctoral degrees in three or more disciplines or 20 or more doctoral degrees in one or more disciplines. Examples include Clarkson University, Dartmouth College, George Mason University, and Michigan Technological University.

Master's (comprehensive) colleges and universities I offer a full range of baccalaureate programs and award 40 or more master's degrees annually in at least three different disciplines. Examples include Bucknell University, Campbell University, and the University of Wisconsin in Plattesville.

Master's (comprehensive) colleges and universities II offer a full range of baccalaureate programs and award 20 or more master's degrees in one or more disciplines. Examples include The Citadel, Susquehanna University, and Hood College.

Baccalaureate (liberal arts) colleges I are primarily undergraduate colleges with major emphasis on baccalaureate degree programs. They are selective in admissions and award 40% or more of the baccalaureate degrees in liberal arts fields. Selectivity is determined by entrance examination scores (SAT or ACT) and class standing. Examples are Vassar College, Davidson College, Guilford College, and Haverford College.

Baccalaureate colleges II are committed to undergraduate education and award fewer than 40% of their undergraduate degrees in liberal arts, and are less restrictive in admissions.

Associate of arts colleges offer associate or arts certificates or degrees, typically in 2 years.

Specialized institutions include theological seminaries, freestanding law schools, teachers colleges, tribal colleges, and others.

Unfortunately, many institutions can fit into more than one category, and there is a great deal of overlap. Another unfortunate spillover from this categorization is that it appears to be hierarchical with the "best" institutions at the top (Research I). The objective of many academic administrators is therefore to move "up" from say Research II to Research I. A starting professor at Ohio State University, for example, was told in no uncertain terms that her primary responsibility was to get research funding and that she should ignore her teaching. Ohio State wants to be among the "elite" Research I universities. But at what cost?

Academic institutions can be classified in many ways. Another useful classification might be the following:

Private research universities have a long history in America, although by European standards our universities are all newcomers. Many early private universities have historical ties to religious denominations, but today most of these universities function as totally independent entities, receiving no assistance from religious organizations. Private research universities often have large medical centers that become the tail that wags the dog. Examples of such secularized institutions are Harvard, Duke, and Stanford.

Public research universities are the public counterpart to private research universities. They have had phenomenal success and growth during the last 50 years. Top examples include the University of North Carolina, University of Michigan, and University of Illinois. The main difference between public and private research institutions is that state-supported schools have a stronger public service component. In state schools, service to the public and not just research is required for promotion and tenure.

Land grant colleges, established during the administration of President Abraham Lincoln, were created to serve the public need for education as well as to transfer knowledge to the public. Many of our largest public research universities started out as land grant colleges and still provide an exemplary and useful service to the public, especially in agricultural extension services. Examples include North Carolina State University, Texas A&M, and Purdue University.

Private comprehensive universities are less competitive in research, offer fewer doctoral programs, and typically do not have large medical research and training facilities. While they often claim to not want to compete with the research universities, their administrators no doubt envy their more famous brothers and would very much like to make the jump to the research university.[2] Examples of such institutions include Carnegie Mellon University, Lehigh University, and Clarkson University.

State-supported teaching universities are in some ways the public analog of the private comprehensive university, and unfortunately they often share the research-over-teaching ambitions. Not willing to take second place in the educational hierarchy, institutions such as Tennessee Technical University or Florida International University, which admirably accomplish their goal of providing excellent education at modest cost to thousands of students, have tried to become research universities. The State of California has developed an entire system of colleges that are supposed to focus on education, but the administrators at many of these campuses chafe at what they often consider their second-class status and want to compete with the more famous research universities.

Private independent liberal arts colleges represent some of the finest teaching and learning experiences to be found anywhere. These exclusive and often expensive institutions provide high-quality instruction and ask little in the way of research from their faculty. Examples include Williams College, Lafayette College, and Swarthmore College.

Private denominationally supported liberal arts colleges include the many Jesuit institutions such as Loyola University in Chicago and Georgetown University. Brigham Young University is the flagship of the Mormon schools, while Liberty University and Bob Jones University are examples of fundamentalist Christian liberal arts colleges.

Urban colleges and universities often have a different tenor to them than the more rural institutions. The troubles as well as excitement of living in a city often affect how research is done and what scholarship is undertaken. Boston University, for example, has taken over running the Boston city school system and uses the schools as a living laboratory for its School of Education. Other examples of urban colleges include the City College of New York, Temple University, and Columbia University.

Military institutes are some of our oldest institutions of higher education in the United States and still play an important role in American education. Examples include the United States Military Academy, as well as private institutions such as Virginia Military Institute and The Citadel.

Private women's colleges emerged around the turn of the century in response to the exclusion of women from higher education. Many of these colleges now also accept men (examples include Sarah Lawrence College, Vassar College, and Beaver College), while others have essentially merged with their all-male counterparts (examples are Radcliffe College and Women's College at Duke University). A few, such as Wellesley College and Cedar Crest College, have remained exclusively colleges for women.

Technical institutes developed independently in America because technology was not considered "education" by early American universities, a bias in part due to the complete separation of universities and technical institutes in Europe. Examples of technical institutes include Massachusetts Institute of Technology, California Institute of Technology, and the Illinois Institute of Technology. Over the years these institutes have evolved into comprehensive universities offering full educational opportunities, but often retain their major focus on technology.

Historically Black colleges and universities (HBCUs) developed as a result of African Americans having been excluded from higher education by various combinations of racism, custom, and economic constraints. Accordingly, universities for and by African Americans developed and often became outstanding institutions now serving students of all races. For the most part, however, they retain their historical African American foundations and this is reflected in their student bodies. Examples of HBCUs include Howard University, Tuskegee University, and North Carolina A&T University.

State-supported teachers colleges have during the past decades almost all changed to universities, defined as any institution that supports more than one college. These institutions continue to provide outstanding educational experiences for students interested in teaching and other service professions at a relatively inexpensive cost to the student. Examples include Slippery Rock University, West Chester State University, and Appalachian State University.

Community colleges and junior colleges are perhaps the fastest growing of the various arms of higher education in the United States. These colleges often offer comprehensive liberal arts education as well as useful vocational training. More technically oriented community colleges offer associate degrees in specific and useful skills such computer technology, auto mechanics, and construction technology.

Correspondence colleges have also seen tremendous growth during the past few decades. People who for diverse reasons did not attend or finish college recognize that job advancement is tied to a college degree, and having no other alternatives, will seek their degrees through correspondence courses. Some correspondence colleges are completely mail oriented (such as Nova University), while others hold classes at various locations in populated areas but rely on correspondence for examinations and other paperwork. Typically, faculty working for these institutions are not full-time but teach on a contractual per-course basis.

The diversity in the types of institutions is reflected in the professional organizations that represent the universities, which are also in semi-chaos. The most prestigious of these organizations is the Association of American Universities (AAU), comprising about 60 research universities which grant about three quarters of all the doctorate degrees in the United States. Only the most productive research universities are asked to join. The American Council on Education (ACE) on the other hand welcomes all colleges and universities. The Association of State Colleges includes all generally non-Ph.D.-granting public institutions, while the National Association of Independent Colleges and Universities serves private colleges and universities.

Obviously it is impossible to list and categorize in any comprehensive way the diversity of American higher education institutions. The main point, however, is that the diversity exists and that this is the strength of the system.

Expectations Differ for Faculties at Different Colleges and Universities

With the wide range of institutions in the American higher education system, the job demands and responsibilities of faculty vary widely. As you plan for an academic career, you must consider the following variables:

Salary. The highest paying institutions are the private research universities—the lowest paying are the junior colleges. Public research universities offer lower pay than private research universities. Medical school faculty are the best paid, followed by the law school. Engineers and accountants often earn higher salaries than humanities professors. If you are interested in average salaries for specific schools, *The Chronicle of Higher Education* publishes an annual summary of faculty salaries for the leading educational institutions.

Teaching versus research. In many colleges you will not be expected to do any research and will not be asked to publish independently. Your job performance will be judged only by your teaching record, together with your service to the community if this is applicable. In research universities, however, the reverse is true. You will be judged almost exclusively on your reputation as a published scholar, and the superstar professors are often required to teach very little, if at all.

Academic freedom. The more scholastically oriented the institution, the more freedom you will have to teach what you want or undertake whatever research interests you. In purely teaching institutions you will often be told in detail what the courses are that you have to cover. If you work for a denominationally supported institution, you must be aware that freedom of thought and expression is often limited. Brigham Young University, for example, requires all of its professors to be certified

Mormons. Without such certification from the Church, you cannot work there. Similarly, don't expect to teach evolutionary biology at Jerry Falwell's Liberty University and hold on to your job for very long.

Mobility. Because American higher education tends to be elitist, the place where you work may affect your ability to move. If you start your career working at a less elite institution, it will be difficult to move up. You will forever be saddled with the question of why you chose to work at that place. Would nobody else hire you? There must be something wrong with you then. The worst scenario is if you fail to make the grade for tenure at a second-rate institution. Time to consider a career with McDonald's. On the other hand, moving down is easier. Faculty who fail to get tenure at an elite institution usually have no trouble finding jobs at less prestigious universities and colleges. The best advice is to shoot for the highest possible position as your initial employment. You can always move down, but upward mobility is limited by the snobbishness of the system.

Part of the problem with starting out at a less prestigious institution is that often teaching loads are great and less time is available for research or scholarship. Often the young professor is saddled with large introductory courses and considerable time is required to prepare the teaching material. A lack of infrastructure such as secretarial support and small grants for summer support increase the problem. Nevertheless, in the humanities and social sciences the publication of several well-regarded books can ensure upward mobility, whereas in the sciences the lack of research opportunity limits mobility.

On the other hand, if your primary interest is *teaching,* then you should seek the best teaching position possible regardless of how prestigious the institution. Some highly ranked places have a terrible teaching environment and most faculty view their teaching chores as the necessary evil that allows them to do research. You might find the commitment to undergraduate education much higher in a small nonresearch or even noncomprehensive school.

Sometimes graduate faculty advisors in the research universities discourage their students from taking jobs in nonresearch institutions because faculty performance at doctoral universities is judged, in part, by how many of their students are eventually employed by the elite research universities. Because more than 80% of all of doctoral degrees in the United States are awarded by only 102 universities, the graduating students often believe that they can only find employment at universities similar to their own, but they should recognize that they have many academic career options in the more than 3,700 diverse colleges and universities.[3]

The mobility of faculty has greatly increased over the years. Not too many years ago professors could plan on spending their entire careers at one institution, but now many senior professors sell their body and mind to the highest bidder. This mobility is acerbated by the universities' custom of asking outside evaluators to judge whether a young professor is tenureable or not. It is very clear that you must impress not only your departmental colleagues, but also your disciplinary soul mates outside of your university. No wonder that in a recent poll, fully 77% of the faculty surveyed declared that their first loyalty was to the discipline, while only 53% felt any loyalty to the institution, and less than 40% of the faculty believed that their department was important.[4]

Teaching load. Because junior colleges do not expect research, their teaching loads are typically the highest, approaching the effort expended by high school teachers. Teaching loads at institutions where research and publication are not required are often three or even four courses a semester. In addition, faculty are expected to do advising and university service. Elite research institutions typically expect three courses a year, provided the faculty are actively pursuing research and seeking external funding. Teaching responsibilities can be eliminated completely if enough research funding is obtained so as to "buy out" of teaching. These faculty will then expect the university (indirectly the students) to support the research. It is a sweet deal for those who are in education to do research.

The Good and the Bad of Choosing an Academic Career[5]

Choosing an academic career is a "consequential decision" in that so much flows from it. Other consequential decisions with equally severe ramifications are choosing a spouse and deciding to have children.[6] So why should you want to make that consequential decision to have a career in higher education? Here are some reasons why you should choose to work at an American institute of higher education:

- Faculties have *academic freedom* to undertake whatever research interests them and to teach the truth as they see it (with exceptions at some denominationally supported institutions).
- Universities, ideally, *serve the public,* not just the wealthy and privileged; being a professor allows you to make this ideal more of a reality.
- What counts in most universities is *merit* and not political pull or affiliation.
- Universities are where people gather to create new knowledge, to foster learning, and to create a *life of the mind* for its participants.
- Universities are mostly *self-governed,* although in some states the politicians try to meddle in the affairs of the university.
- The greatest joy in universities is to *teach young minds* and to watch these people develop into productive adults.
- University life allows for a *flexible schedule,* with large chunks of time for research and scholarly activity.
- Most universities will give *sabbatical leaves.* Usually a professor can get one semester with no responsibilities at full pay for every 7 years of service, or an entire year at half salary. If you can find someone to pay half your salary you can be off campus for more than a year. Overseas opportunities are available and can make for extended intellectual and educational experiences for you and your family.
- The *intellectual resources* of a university are unlimited.
- Universities are driven by *honor* and high standards.
- Being a member of a university faculty means that you are in *good company.* Your friends and colleagues are also honorable people with keen minds doing interesting things they want to share with you.

There are, however, some less attractive attributes about universities as well.

- Academic freedom can result in some faculty becoming *eccentrics* and *exhibitionists.*

- Academic freedom and the pressure to publish can also lead some faculty to conduct *useless research and scholarship,* research that is of little if any interest or use by society.
- Faculty, because of their exalted position, tend to want to raise the drawbridge and not change their privileged life, becoming increasingly *conservative* in their thinking. Getting a faculty to make substantive modifications in a curriculum is often like turning ocean liners.
- *Overspecialization* has created insulated and insular fiefdoms in universities where the professors do not interact with their colleagues within the university, but rather with their professional soul mates at other universities. The result is a fractured faculty often unable to agree on anything.
- Because it is imperative to impress colleagues outside of the university with one's scholarly credentials, and because many colleagues do not know or care about classroom activities, *good teaching is not rewarded* and *bad teaching is tolerated.*
- Professors can be *mean-spirited* and nasty, fighting for trivial advantage. As the old saying goes, "Academic politics are so vicious because the stakes are so small."
- Because so much of a professor's life is dependent on a voluntary sharing of duties, some professors don't participate in service either outside or inside the university. Community-minded professors often bear an *uneven share* of these burdens.
- A *lack of interest by the faculty* in either teaching or university governance creates a power vacuum that can be filled by amoral, and even immoral, academic administrators interested only in personal advancement and self-enrichment.
- Some faculty use the university as a means of *enriching themselves,* setting up private companies with university time and resources.

Generally, people who work in colleges and universities are well satisfied with their jobs. The Higher Education Research Institute recently did a survey on job satisfaction, the results of which are shown in Table 1.1.

The most important conclusion from this table is that there appears to be job satisfaction at an equal rate at all institutions regardless of classification. Universities tend to allow more time for scholarly pursuits,

TABLE 1.1 Job Satisfaction by Instructional Type

Percentage of Respondents Being "Very Satisfied" or "Satisfied"

		Universities		Four-Year Colleges		Two-Year Colleges	
	All	*Public*	*Private*	*Public*	*Private*	*Public*	*Private*
Overall job satisfaction	70	65	72	67	72	77	72
Autonomy and independence	83	84	86	80	85	82	78
Undergraduate courses	78	77	78	76	80	80	75
Professional relationships with other faculty	72	67	70	71	75	77	80
Graduate courses	71	74	74	68	70	49	50
Job security	71	70	71	69	68	76	65
Competency of colleagues	67	63	70	65	72	70	74
Working conditions	66	67	75	63	67	64	61
Social relationships with other faculty	61	55	61	60	62	66	72
Relationships with the administration	54	50	54	54	57	54	60
Teaching load	52	60	58	47	48	49	46
Opportunity for scholarly pursuits	45	52	52	38	42	44	37
Salary and fringe benefits	41	32	50	28	43	50	42
Quality of students	39	37	59	38	47	31	30
Visibility for jobs at other institutions/organizations	39	41	46	35	38	39	38

SOURCE: Dey, E. L., Ramirez, C. E., Korn, W. S., & Astin, A. W. (1993). *The American college teacher*. Los Angeles: Higher Education Research Institute, University of California at Berkeley.

and faculty at private universities seem to be better satisfied with their salaries than their colleagues at public universities, although this is reversed for the two-year colleges. The single largest difference occurs in the quality of students. Faculty at private universities are twice as satisfied with the quality of their students as faculty at two-year colleges. None of these results come as a great surprise, of course. What this survey indicates is that on balance, all faculty, regardless of the type of institution, seem to be fairly well satisfied with their jobs and careers.

Personally, I believe that there is nothing like an academic career! Few are the people who can say that they have the best job in the world, and I can honestly say I do. Sure, there are jerks everywhere, from departmental chairs to deans to provosts to presidents and everything in between, and there are times when your colleagues leave you exasperated and even angry, but most of them are good and honorable people trying to do the very best job they can. The opportunities for self-advancement and intellectual growth are unlimited. You don't have to punch a time clock and you can do your work when it suits you. And most important, the opportunity to work with students in molding their characters and providing them an educational foundation is unparalleled, despite the problems. It *is* a great career choice and I highly recommend it.

Notes

1. Carnegie Foundation for the Advancement of Teaching. (1994). *A classification of institutions of higher education* (pp. 15-17). Princeton, NJ: Author.

2. Sometimes this quest results in disappointment and disillusionment. As so aptly put, "By believing themselves to be what they are not, institutions fall short of being what they could be." (Ernest Lynton and Sandra Elman, 1987, *New priorities for the university*. San Francisco: Jossey-Bass, p. 13).

3. Gaff, J. G., & Lambert, L. M. (1996). Socializing future faculty to the values of undergraduate education. *Change* (July/August), 38-46.

4. Boyer, E. (1990). *Scholarship reconsidered: Priorities of the professorate*. Princeton, NJ: Carnegie Foundation for Advancement of Education.

5. Some of these points are also listed in Schoenfeld, A. C., & Magan, R. (1992). *Mentor in a manual*. Madison, WI: Magna.

6. Reis, R. (1997). *Tomorrow's professor: Preparing for academic careers in science and engineering*. Piscataway, NJ: IEEE.

CHAPTER 2

Getting an Academic Job

Where is the line forming for all those universities that want to have you on their faculty?

There is no such line, and given the increasing glut of terminal degree graduates, it is unlikely that this will soon change. *To get hired, you have to sell yourself.*

In this chapter, I first look at the decision that science Ph.D.s have to face: to post-doc or not to post-doc. Then I discuss how universities decide to hire someone and the criteria they use to make such a decision. Next I describe where academic job openings are listed and where you can learn of these openings, and then I argue that the most important factor in being hired is how you present yourself. Throughout this chapter I consider the search process from the perspective of the hiring university to illustrate how you will be judged and who will do that judging.

To Post-Doc or Not to Post-Doc?

After the Ph.D., should you do an apprenticeship period, the "post-doc"? This depends on many factors, including the availability of tenure-track jobs, the availability of good post-doc positions, and the conventional route to success within a field. In the humanities, formal post-docs are rare, although many graduating Ph.D.s take positions that are nontenure track in order to provide them time to get their scholarly work into print and to find the time to seek just the right position. In the natural sciences, a post-doc is becoming increasingly important if the aim is to work at a research university. Post-docs allow you to work for a limited time in another laboratory and to get to know a whole new group of people, many of whom will be your peers during your career. Having had a post-doc position with a particularly well-known scientist will almost guarantee you a good starting assistant professor position at a research university. But if your aim is to work in the less elite institutions, then post-docs are certainly not necessary and might be a waste of time (and money, since post-docs are paid considerably less than starting assistant professors).

If you want to do a post-doc, you should find a position at the most elite institution possible. Such institutions will have many applications from which to choose. From their point of view, the best post-doc is one who has accomplished something in a reasonable time. That is, the Ph.D. has not taken too long, because, after all, the post-doc will be for only a year or two, and something should be accomplished within that short time. The post-doc must also be a good presenter of his or her research and must be able to present the results of the laboratory group with distinction. Finally, the post-doc must be a person who will make friends quickly and interact with the laboratory group.

From your perspective, you will need to find a place where you know you can accomplish something significant within a year or two. You want to finish a project, not just work on something. After starting the post-doc position, you will be out on the job search trail almost immediately, and the sooner you can demonstrate effective finished work, the better. Do not sign on to a 2-year post-doc where the project is to take 4 years to finish.

A second variable in selecting the post-doc position is the person for whom you would be working. You want to have the laboratory director become your supporter and mentor for the long haul, and you want this person to be someone who can help your career.

The process of applying for post-docs is fairly simple. Most post-doc positions are obtained by the old-boy network. If you want a post-doc, talk to your Ph.D. advisor, and he or she will send out letters to various colleagues attesting to your research skills and explaining how you will win the Nobel Prize within the next few years. Alternatively, you can apply independently, but you must be aware that your Ph.D. advisor will be called and asked for an assessment of your talents and skills. Because the post-doc position is not a permanent faculty or staff position, the recruitment and hiring are fairly informal.

Choosing Where to Apply for a Tenure-Track Job

If your choice is to seek a tenure-track job immediately after graduation, the job search process is very different and much more complex and depends very much on the type of university or college you are applying to. An excellent source of addresses and other information on American universities is the *Higher Education Directory*.[1]

Be aware that you will most likely not be hired by the research university from which you received your degree. Most newly minted Ph.D.s will not go to work in universities resembling the ones from which they graduated. Fewer than 10% of Ph.D.s from research universities will in fact end up in research universities. One well-regarded university recently awarded 419 doctorates in the arts, humanities, and social sciences during a 3-year period, and only 25 of these went on to obtain faculty positions at other research universities.[2]

In selecting a university in which to apply, one sure characteristic that you will want to consider is the quality of the students, both undergraduate and graduate. You have to match your own interests and abilities to the students with whom you will be working. If your yen is to do high-quality research, then a community college would not be appropriate. You will find at community colleges students who are far behind in their reading and mathematical skills and who will not be able to participate in your work. On the other hand, most of us don't need a class of superbrights to have fun teaching and doing good research. The main thing is that you want students who are interested and willing to learn and from whose successes you will draw satisfaction and reward.

Your two major variables in selecting candidate universities will be the amount and type of teaching you will do and whether you will be

TABLE 2.1 Contact Hours (Teaching and Laboratory) in Private Four-Year Universities

Contact Hours per Week	Percentage of Faculty
Less than 5	5
5 to 8	18
8 to 12	47
13 to 16	20
More than 16	10

SOURCE: Dey, E. L., Ramirez, C. E., Korn, W. S., & Astin, A. W. (1993). *The American college teacher.* Los Angeles: Higher Education Research Institute, UCLA.

TABLE 2.2 Climate for Research at Various Universities

Teaching Colleges			Research Colleges	Research Universities
Tolerant	Welcoming	Supporting		
Allow research	Welcome research	Encourage research	Expect research	Require research
Do not encourage with funds and time	Do not encourage with funds and time	Encourage with funds and time	Encourage with funds and time	Encourage with funds and time
			Encourage external grants	Demand external grants
Not considered for tenure and promotion	Not considered for tenure and promotion	Influential for tenure and promotion	Important for tenure and promotion	Crucial for tenure and promotion

SOURCE: Gibson, G. W. (1992). *Good start* (p. 132). Bolton, MA: Anker.

expected to do research or participate in scholarly activity. The amount of time spent in class and laboratory (contact hours) can vary tremendously depending on your own interests and the institution. A recent survey of private 4-year colleges showed that the hours per week scheduled for classes can vary, as shown in Table 2.1.

If your university requires more than 16 contact hours per week, there will be little time left over for research or writing.

The encouragement and support of research also varies widely, as noted in Table 2.2.

Salary

What motivates us to become teachers? Gibson suggests that many future professors might have the following dream(s):[3]

- *The Evangelist dream:* a desire to advance the ideals of liberal learning
- *The Maestro dream:* a wish to be appreciated as a disciplinary expert
- *The Mentor dream:* a desire to contribute to the intellectual and personal development of students
- *The Thespian dream:* a yearning to enrapture audiences with impeccable performances
- *The Goldfinger dream:* the longing to create one's own world and to rule over it

Gibson does *not* include

- *The Midas dream*: the longing to be wealthy.

If the Midas dream is your dream, you are in the wrong business. As a young assistant professor, you cannot expect to be paid very much. Highest professorial salaries, in the range of $60,000, go to professors of accounting and to medical researchers, followed by engineers and lawyers. A starting assistant engineering professor at an elite research university can expect to be offered $50,000. But by far the greatest number of assistant professors will receive salaries in the range of $35,000 to $40,000.

The salary you can expect will vary according to the geographic location, with the New England colleges usually having the highest salaries, followed by mid-Atlantic and Pacific regions. The south-central region typically has the lowest salaries.[4]

Other Considerations

Although the selection of a university is often not based on rational calculations, it is nevertheless useful to take a shot at rationality. Below is a method for comparing several offers, or for deciding where to apply.[5]

Begin by rating the attributes that are important to you, rate these by importance on a scale of 1 to 5, and then rate the actual characteristic at the university. For example, if the importance of a strong research program is vitally important to you, rate this as 5. If you are choosing between Duke University and Williams College, the university characteristic for a strong research program for Duke is 5, while for Williams it would be 1. If a collegial atmosphere within your department is somewhat important, you might rate this attribute as 4. You might have bad feelings about the way people get along at the Duke department and thus rate its characteristic as 2, while the faculty at Williams seem to be genuinely interested in supporting each other and getting along as colleagues, so you rate that characteristic for Williams as 5. A third attribute might be the size of the school. Suppose this is not very important to you, so the importance rating is one. The actual characteristic of Duke in terms of size would be 4 and Williams 2. The first three lines might then be:

		Duke		Williams	
		Characteristic		Characteristic	
Attribute	*Importance*				
	(I)	*(C)*	*C x I*	*(C)*	*C x I*
Strong research	5	5	25	1	5
Collegiality	4	2	8	5	20
Size	1	4	4	2	2
Total			37		27

You can then add up the C x I columns for the different schools and have a numerical comparison of your options, whether real or ideal. The attributes can be made up, depending on what you feel is important to you. Here is a partial list of those that you might want to consider:

1. Research and publishing is how success is measured.
2. Excellence in teaching is valued and rewarded.
3. The school has a strong religious association.
4. The size of the school is comfortable to me.
5. The school has a highly selective student body.
6. The school has both graduate and undergraduate programs.

7. Given my background and experience, I have a strong chance of getting tenure.

8. The departmental faculty has established a collegial and supportive environment.

9. The dean and the department chair are respected and liked by the faculty.

10. If I will be the first person of my race, gender, or national background in the department, I will be accepted as a colleague.

11. The age distribution of the department faculty will not force me to compete for tenure and promotion with my peers.

12. I can expect to find a mentor who will help me get started.

13. The location of the campus is urban/rural.

14. Transportation to the nearest airport is easy.

15. Parking is easy, cheap, and convenient.

16. I like the school colors.

17. The school has a generous sabbatical program, especially for junior faculty.

18. The salary is competitive.

19. I will get the lab space I will need.

20. I will receive substantial start-up funding.

21. Benefits, including health, retirement, and tuition for children, are competitive.

22. The library is adequate and accessible.

23. Computational facilities are adequate.

24. The offer includes moving expenses.

25. I can be proud to be part of this academic enterprise.

Of course, this is not a complete list. You can add or subtract as appropriate. Most people will make such consequential decisions with their hearts, so don't expect the tabulation to make up your mind for you. The exercise will, however, point out some areas that you might otherwise not have considered.

Applying for a Job While Holding the ABD

There is a time in every Ph.D. student's career when he or she begins to despair. The courses are done, the prelims are taken, and the research has begun. But the end is so very far away. And being poor is not fun. Why not get an academic job somewhere and finish the dissertation at your own pace? After all, you have the topic, you know the procedure, and all you have to do is hunker down and get it done.

I am in full sympathy with this temptation. But the statistics (if they exist) must be staggering against ever finishing the Ph.D. once you leave the university. Picture the situation: You have just finished a grueling day of teaching, advising, and other stuff, and you must now come home to your domestic chores. At 9 p.m. you finally have some free time, but you are bushed. There is no energy, either physical or mental. So you bag it for the night and go to bed. You do that again and again, and the unfinished dissertation gets more and more remote in your mind. Eventually, you recognize that if you are to get to it again, you will need a large block of time, like a month, to get back up to speed. You don't have that month, so you put it off again. Eventually, you resign yourself to never finishing it, place it in the back of your bureau drawer, and occasionally look at it with deep regret. This is such a common scenario that the field has given such people a semi-serious degree designation, "All But Dissertation"—the ABD.

Most universities will have high ethical standards and will not hire anyone with an ABD to a tenure-track position. They know that more than likely they will be destroying a career by encouraging the young person to go to work without finishing the dissertation. Other universities are not so ethical and will take ABD people, giving them some lower rank such as "Instructor" and chewing them up, telling them all along that when the degree is finished they will be promoted to Assistant Professor. It is an insidious process. They know full well that only a small fraction of the ABDs will actually finish, and in the meantime they have a cheap faculty member whom they can fire at any time.

In short, do not even *think* about getting the ABD and going to work. Are you really that special, that you have the willpower that tens of thousands of others lack? If you are Wonder Woman or Superman, go ahead. All others—stick it out and get your degree first.

The Job Opening

Every college and university is different in its governance. Some department chairs have the power to hire, while at other universities that decision is made by the vice president for academic affairs, commonly called the provost. Most likely, the decision to hire a new faculty member is made by a lower administrator such as a departmental chair, who then asks a higher administrator such as a dean to allow for a new hire. The key factor is the source of the money. If the money for the new hire's salary comes from the dean of the school, it is ultimately his or her decision. If departments are on strict budgets, then the chair makes the decision.

Assuming that the dean decides, on what basis is this decision made? As with many things academic, the decision is clouded in mystery and personal prejudice (and perhaps ambition). A forceful departmental chair might convince the dean that the teaching load in the department is too high and that the teaching is suffering and/or a mutiny is brewing among the faculty. Most deans will listen to such pleas. Some will not.

One source of pressure to relieve teaching loads might come from the accreditation reports.[6] If the accreditation is in jeopardy, the dean will have to listen and respond by hiring new faculty. But this argument works only where the accreditation is really in jeopardy. If the program is solid and everything is going well except that the faculty are overloaded, then the accreditation agency cannot influence the hiring of new faculty.

Finally, the decision to hire new faculty might be based on the ambitions of the dean. New faculty can bring in new overhead money,[7] and since the overhead money stays with the dean, the dean has money to use for other purposes. With this money, he or she can hire new faculty, renovate buildings, buy computers, and so on. In most cases, the dean will use this money to build more laboratories or purchase equipment for research, hoping to entice more faculty to bring in even more external funding so that even more overhead money will be available and so on. The purpose of this pyramid scheme is not to improve the learning and teaching environment for undergraduate students, because these research faculty will seldom participate in the instructional program. Rather, the increased visibility of the research program would be expected to yield higher rankings in *U.S. News and World Report* and other such evaluations. Figuring prominently in these calculations is the total research funding for the school; thus, the external funding directly affects the ranking (and an increase in the rankings of course proves that the dean is a great academic administrator).

The decision to advertise for a new position is a complex process, and you as the potential job candidate may never know how it came to be. It is, however, terribly important to know who will ultimately decide on the hiring. If you know who the "buyer" is, you can do a better job of "selling" yourself by emphasizing to the buyer those attributes that make you most attractive as a potential hire.

The Job Notice

Typically, the search for a faculty position begins with a departmental chair appointing a search committee. Sometimes the chair heads the committee, but often the chair will appoint someone else to do the work. The committee, with the concurrence of the chair and often the dean, writes the job notice and posts it in the relevant publications. The committee members may also start a word-of-mouth process by calling or writing their fellow scholars at other universities asking if they have any bright graduate students on the verge of graduating. They may also send individual letters to faculty in their specific fields bringing to their attention the job opening. Their objective is to make the opening as widely known as possible.

You no doubt have a good idea what publications carry the job notices for your profession. The largest such publication is the *Chronicle of Higher Education,* published every other week. It carries notices for all fields with the exception of the professional schools such as engineering, law, and medicine. Notices for job openings in professional schools appear in the respective professional publications. Each discipline also has a special service for listing job openings. For example, the American Historical Society has a newsletter that lists openings, as well as an email listserv. The environmental engineering field lists its openings on a home page, as well as in a quarterly newsletter. Find out from your mentor how to access all these sources. A listing of some of the Web sites you can use for a job search appears in the appendix at the end of this chapter.

The way the job notice is written may give you some clue as to whether or not you should even bother applying. Equal opportunity laws require all job vacancies to be publicized, even if the job is already wired—that is, the decision has already been made. One clue to wired ads is the specificity of the job description. If it says, for example, that the job in the history department requires someone who is a specialist in the history of the buggy whip industry, there may be only one person in the entire world who can claim to be such a specialist, and it is clear that he or she is the designated recipient of that job offer.

A different kind of problem arises when the notice is written in such vague terms that you have no idea what kind of person they are looking for. This could be because the person writing the notice is inept, or because the department is on a fishing expedition to see what is out there and who responds. A well-written job announcement indicates that the department has carefully considered the appointment and is taking the search seriously.

The job notice should be specific but not overly so. It should also say if the position is for assistant, associate, or full professor, or if the rank is open. Finally, it should specify the dates of the search, what the deadline for application will be and when the decision will be made. A job notice without a deadline might suggest that the department is having difficulties in recruiting faculty.

Most important, before you decide to apply (and encumber your recommenders with yet another letter to write on your behalf), you should run the idea past your advisor/mentor. People in the field have a good sense of where you would fit best with your interests and abilities and can give you sage advice. They can also steer you away from troubled programs. No sense in jumping into a snake pit for your first job.

The Application

In response to the job notice, you want to send, at a minimum, your résumé and a cover letter stating why you want the job and why you think you are the most qualified person for it.

The résumé should be concise, accurate, and attractive. You should put the most important things first. If you are applying for an academic job, your academic credentials should be listed immediately after your name and address (snail mail, fax, telephone, and email). Next you should list your publications, including publications that have been submitted but not yet accepted. Do not, however, list the ones you are only thinking

TABLE 2.3 Items for Your Résumé

	Required	Optional	Special Circumstance
Personal information			
Name	x		
Address, home and office	x		
Telephone, home and office	x		
Email address	x		
Date of birth		x	
Place of birth		x	
Marital status		x	
Religious affiliation			x
Educational history			
Degrees (and honors)	x		
Year degrees obtained	x		
Other education (no degrees)	x		
Ph.D. dissertation title	x		
Ph.D. dissertation advisor		x	
Honors and awards			
Honor societies	x		
Scholarships and fellowships	x		
Professional registration	x		

of writing. You may be asked for copies of these publications and it would be truly embarrassing to say that they do not yet exist.

Table 2.3 is a checklist of items for your résumé.

Relevant work experience is good, especially if it is in the field. Engineering faculty, for example, want to see that you have had some practical experience and could become a registered professional engineer, since the accreditation agencies beat on the departments to have faculty with professional engineering licenses.

There are two controversial issues. The first is whether or not to include a picture on your résumé.

I believe a picture is worth a lot, and there is nothing unseemly, illegal, or immoral about including a picture. You can get really nice

TABLE 2.3 Continued

	Required	Optional	Special Circumstance
Language facility		x	x
Work experience			
Firms or companies	x		
Title of jobs held and years	x		
Responsibilities		x	
Publications			
Full-length refereed papers	x		
Books	x		
Other publications	x		
Presentations			
Oral presentations	x		
Poster sessions	x		
Proceedings papers	x		
Research interests		x	
Teaching interests			x
References	x		

SOURCE: Based in part on Gibson, G. (1992). *Good start* (p. 39). Bolton, MA: Anker.

résumé front pages done at a copy center using color copying. The résumé is, after all, you in print. Why not have a picture of yourself as well as a list of your accomplishments? I do not know of any reasons to the contrary except that, traditionally, résumés do not include pictures.

On the other hand, there may be fields (such as anthropology) where a picture on a résumé is totally unacceptable and can be considered bad manners or worse. It is best to speak to your advisor about this before making a decision on including a picture.

The second controversial issue is whether to include a list of references.

The answer is absolutely *yes*. The only reason you would not want to include them is that you are in industry and are fishing for a job, and you might not want your colleagues and especially your bosses to know that you are in the market for a new job. By saying "references on request" on your résumé, you have control over when to give out the names. If you are in industry and a firm to which you have sent your résumé turns out to be an unattractive option for you, you do not jeopardize your standing with your present firm by having your bosses receive requests for references. You simply decline to give out the names of your references. But when you are a graduate student, everyone knows that you are seeking a position. Why not include the names of the professors who already have agreed to be your references? They will probably welcome the opportunity to help you find a good job. Putting "references on request" on your résumé seems arrogant and unnecessary.

Selecting your references is an important decision. Ideally, you want a few Nobel laureates to say that you are the most brilliant person on earth. Failing that, you should select your references in order to provide the most positive picture of your past successes and future potential. The strongest case would be made if you can have several senior faculty in the department write reference letters. A letter from a senior scholar is a strong statement because the potential employer assumes that the writer has little to gain by overemphasizing your positive attributes and would not risk his or her standing as a colleague by false praise (or the omission of relevant negative facts).

From your standpoint, I would choose those faculty with whom you have the strongest rapport. They know you the best and would be able to write informed and informative letters. Finally, they have a stake in your professional success and will take the time and trouble to work on writing the best possible letters.

If the job is in a research university, your application must also include a statement of research interests. Be sure to talk to your mentor about how to write the statement of research interests. Ask how best to package your statement so it will appeal to the dean, who is no doubt seeking research funding and who will evaluate you as a potential revenue producer. If your statement tells the dean that you are planning to work in a hot, funding-rich area, you have an immediate advantage. If you tell the dean, on the other hand, that you want to work in an area that presently receives no external support, don't get your hopes up. Obviously, if you have already been a part of a research project and obtained funding on your own, you have a tremendous advantage over other applicants. As a graduate student, make obtaining funding one of your priorities to prepare for the job market.

Such funding in sciences would be grants that you help write with your mentor. In the humanities and social sciences, the funding might be in the form of short-term grants for doing special projects or for working on your dissertation. Travel grants from foundations, for example, are excellent examples of your entrepreneurial spirit and your willingness to seek external funding. In addition, faculty who have to make a decision among several excellent candidates will be swayed by the fact that other reviewers and judges have already found what you wrote to be of sufficient value to give you money. Hence, money/awards beget money/awards.[8]

In addition to the research interests statement, you should include a statement of your teaching experience and interests. If you are applying to a research university do not say that your *primary* objective in an academic career is to be a good teacher. Remember, the dean of a research university often does not care whether you are or are not a good teacher, but cares very much whether or not you will most likely bring in research money.

If you are applying to a teaching college, the teaching interests statement will be your most important selling tool. This statement should include a short commentary on your philosophy as a teacher—how you approach the process of teaching and what you have learned already as a graduate student. You should list the courses you have taught or assisted in and what role you had in each. Include a syllabus and any other material the evaluators might find useful. Remember that only a small minority of the 3,700 educational institutions in the United States emphasize research. The great majority will place undergraduate teaching as the top institutional priority, and your success in undergraduate teaching will be an important criterion in finding a suitable job.

During the past few years, entrepreneurial graduate students have begun to dress up their applications by combining their résumé and statements into a *teaching and research portfolio* (see Table 2.4). The portfolio can contain a personal statement about research and teaching, copies of student comments on your teaching, descriptions of awards you might have won, overseas experiences (especially important in the humanities), or industrial employment (especially important in engineering).

TABLE 2.4 What Might be Included in Your Teaching and
Research Portfolio

Teaching

Most Important

- Written classroom observation reports from faculty supervisors
- Statement about your teaching philosophy and personal teaching goals
- End-of-course student evaluations
- Written reflections of teaching evaluations
- Teaching awards and recognition

Important

- Course/lab/recitations section syllabi
- Special teaching-related projects, materials, or curricula authored
- Descriptions of courses previously taught (or ones you are qualified to teach)
- Mid-course student evaluations
- Evidence of participation in teaching-related sessions at conferences and disciplinary society meetings
- A summary statement from a faculty mentor
- Evidence of foreign travel and language capability

Useful

- Sample student essays, papers, and class projects
- Videotapes of classroom teaching
- Unsolicited testimony from students

Research, Scholarship, and Creative Accomplishments

Most Important

- External funding secured to conduct research or scholarship
- Statement of future research agendas or creative work
- Reprints or preprints of published articles or book chapters
- Honors and recognition in research and creative endeavors

Copies of published papers and the abstract from your dissertation would be prominently included. The structure of a portfolio allows you to be imaginative and creative with your application and will set your submission apart from the rest.

If you decide to use a portfolio, here are some tips that might make the job easier and more rewarding.[9]

TABLE 2.4 Continued

Important

- Research presented at conferences of scholarly/disciplinary societies
- Invited seminars at your own and other universities
- Peer reviews of scholarly/creative work
- Notices of juried exhibitions
- Service to an academic society as a journal editor, manuscript reviewer, or conference paper reviewer

Useful

- Descriptions of service as a peer reviewer for research grant competitions
- Evidence of your mentoring or apprentices in research and creative endeavors who have gone on to achieve success of their own

Service

Most Important

- Descriptions of service to university and departmental committees
- Participation in university governance

Important

- Administrative service to department, college, or university
- Service to professional/disciplinary society or organizations
- National service such as the Peace Corps or Teach America

Useful

- Community service related to university position
- Service to local schools
- Volunteer tutoring
- (In special cases) volunteer work for religious organizations

---

- Start compiling samples for your portfolio as soon as possible.
- Form the habit of filing away samples of work that illustrate your teaching.
- Select those items that you deem to be the best examples of your work demonstrating teaching quality.
- The format of a teaching portfolio will vary, depending on intended use.

- Be sure the format is well organized and presents your work with care, neatness, and creativity.
- After you secure a job, plan to continue to retain copies of your work.

A particularly good book on portfolio construction is *The Teaching Portfolio—Capturing the Scholarship of Teaching* (1991), by Russell Edgerton, Patricia Hutchings, and Kathleen Quinlan, which can be obtained from the American Association of Higher Education, Washington, D.C.

The Screening

Your letter of application is received by the department, and a departmental secretary organizes all the applications into file folders. You will receive a friendly form letter from the search committee chair acknowledging the receipt of your application. Your dossier will receive a number and will then sit quietly in a file drawer.

At some appointed time, the search committee starts to look through these dossiers. This is the most critical time for your application. A typical search attracts hundreds of applications. There is no way the search committee can read them all in detail. By necessity, quick decisions are made, often on the basis of the university from which you have graduated, whether or not you have any publications, and who your mentor is. Here, the *visual presentation* of your material is important. If your application stands out as thoughtfully prepared, it will have a much better chance of making the cut than a sloppily and carelessly assembled application. If your dossier does not make it past this cursory review, don't blame your research statement, your teaching statement, or the letters of recommendation. The committee may never have read your statements and most certainly would not have sent for letters of recommendation.

If the job is a teaching position, the initial screening often will be based on experience. Often the announcement will say unequivocally that they do not seek people with great potential in teaching, but rather want to look at people with demonstrated excellence. You have to have proof that you can do it, not just enthusiasm and willingness to be a good teacher.

There is another way you can influence the initial screening process: You may know some of the faculty in the department before you send in your application. These reviewers can then place a name with a face, and, if they have been favorably impressed by the face, they will choose your dossier for further review. The best way to meet people is to attend and participate in professional conferences.

Attending a professional conference gives you your first opportunity to engage in the age-old practice of networking—the "who-you-know" method of employment and promotion. The "who-you-know" factor is very important to the faculty seeking to hire a young colleague. If a senior person is trying to make difficult decisions about young faculty, a personal knowledge about the person—placing a face with a résumé—is extremely helpful. Networking of course does not have to be direct. In indirect networking a prospective employer asks for information from trustworthy peers. If these professional colleagues have good things to say about a candidate, then the level of confidence in a positive (or sometimes negative) decision is greatly enhanced. Your objective is, therefore, to be in a position where such positive information can be shared among faculty and colleagues. You can greatly improve your networking effectiveness by following some rules suggested by Heiberger and Vick.[10]

Before a conference, find out which faculty members from your department will attend and ask them to introduce you to the people you would like to meet. Submit a paper or poster session, and do a good job with the presentation. Dress conservatively and wear your name tag. Do not assume people will remember you. Attend sessions that interest you, ask questions from the audience, and/or talk with the speakers afterward. Participate in smaller interest groups that may have meetings apart from the main conference. Some organizations, for example, have active women's groups. If possible, take part in informal social gatherings attended by members of your department and faculty from other institutions. Do not stray too far from your mentor, and take the opportunity to be introduced to his or her colleagues. Do not be bashful. Introduce yourself. If possible, stay in the hotel that is hosting the main conference. This will give you the greatest opportunity to meet the people you wish to get to know, and this in turn will give your application the best chance to be elected for further review. View networking in a positive light.

Networking shares information, and information in making job decisions is always beneficial.

Suppose your dossier has survived the first (unkind) cut. It now gets placed in a pile of perhaps 25 to 50 applications that will be scrutinized further. Now the committee members read your research statement (and, in the case of teaching colleges, your teaching interests statement), and they evaluate your other accomplishments. From this second round emerges a short list of perhaps five to eight candidates that the committee recommends to the departmental chair. Depending on who does the hiring, the chair may share these dossiers with the dean.

In some cases, the committee chair sends letters to the references of the five to eight candidates, asking for their comments. At this point, your references can hurt your chances by not replying in a timely fashion. The search committee is confident that all of the letters will be excellent, but some letters may include items you might have neglected to mention, such as how well you get along with others, how much initiative you take, whether or not you have good table manners, and so on.

Important here is the torpedo letter. Because you have chosen these references yourself, the search committee has every expectation that your handpicked referees will send good letters. But what if one or more of them are lukewarm or even negative? Deadly. This does happen occasionally, and there appears to be no easy way of eliminating this possibility. There is, however, a way of reducing the potential that your references include a short, curt letter that does little to explain your qualifications. Such an unhelpful letter can be construed to mean that the writer simply did not have any enthusiasm for writing the letter or does not think well of you. You can help here by handing to the writer a one-page summary of your activities and qualifications from which he or she can construct the letter. Often the writer will want to say something nice, but in the rush of multiple responsibilities simply cannot think of anything. Your summary will be of great help. But avoid the temptation to give them "suggested" letters. Not only is this bad form, but there is a danger that more than one of your reference writers will use the same sentences in their letters, forcing the readers to question the veracity of the letters (and your honesty).

Based on the recommendation of the search committee and the letters of the references, the controller of the funds then decides which applicants should be interviewed. The departmental chair then sends letters of invitation to the four or five applicants who have made the second cut.

This also brings up an interesting ethical problem. Suppose you were not invited to visit and you want to know the reason. You call the chair of the search committee and ask for clarification. For many reasons, most notably the need to maintain confidentiality, the chair will not tell you the truth. Suppose, for example, you have negative reference letters. For the search committee chair to say that your letters were not positive would be the truth, but it would also breach confidentiality. You know who your letter writers were, and you will know that at least one of them wrote a negative letter. This would be valuable knowledge for the future, but it would poison your relationship with your professors/mentors. Most likely, the chair of the search committee will be noncommittal and say something like "overall evaluations identified stronger candidates," which leaves you in the dark but preserves the confidentiality of the system. As good utilitarians, we sacrifice the occasional individual to prevent the destruction of a basically good system.

The Interview

In some disciplines, the first interview takes place at a professional conference. In English and foreign languages, for example, the professional conventions are used as a means of interviewing potential job candidates without having to pay for them to visit the university. The Modern Language Association (MLA) runs a formal job interview process as part of its annual convention. Following the submission of your letter and résumé to a university, the first response you might get is an invitation to come to such an interview at the annual convention. Sometimes the invitation will include the place and time for the interview, or the letter will let you know where you can sign up for interview times.

The interview is conducted by a group of faculty who may or may not have the foggiest notion how to conduct an effective interview. You will be asked to come into the room and will then be quizzed. You should bring extra copies of your résumé and copies of other work that you might want to share with the interviewers. (Remember to keep all the important things with you on the airplane and not put them in your checked luggage.) Let the interviewers ask the initial questions, but then make sure you get your turn at bat. Ask about the job and the university, demonstrating the understanding of the situation that you have gleaned from the Web. Be confident but not arrogant. Shake hands. Wear nice clothes, but do not overdress.

After your conference interview, or a review of your dossier, suppose you have made the short list and are asked to come visit the university. Although it often goes unsaid, this is a free trip for you. After your visit, gather all your expenses, including the original receipt for your airfare and hotel bill, and send these to the department. But do not charge hotel movies! Typically you arrange your own travel, and the host arranges for the hotel. It is good manners for the host to tell you to send your receipts to him or her after your return, but if they do not, you might want to ask to make sure that the trip expenses will be reimbursed.

You will be met at the airport (if it is a class act) or told how to get to your hotel. One member of the search committee will be your host and will meet you at the hotel or airport and will have your itinerary (unless they have already sent it to you in the mail—another nice touch by classy folks). The itinerary will outline the people you will see and the places you will be. You will no doubt be asked to present a seminar, as well as see some administrative VIPs such as the dean and provost.

So you are ready to start the grueling day. What to wear?

For people of the male persuasion, I recommend a sport coat, white shirt, and subdued (not flashy) tie. Don't overdress. Professors are pretty informal folks, and you don't want to stand out like a Brooks Brothers model. But equally beware of underdressing. You are, after all, on display, and you don't want to look like a slob. Get a haircut (or at least comb your hair), clean your fingernails, and do all the things your mother told you to do.

For women, the same general advice applies. You want to be comfortable but not informal. Remember that the faculty are thinking "How do I feel about working with this person for the next 30 years?" A business suit is appropriate. Sandals and tank tops are unacceptable.

One other thing before you begin your day: You should have done some homework before the trip, looking through the catalogs and the home pages on the World Wide Web to familiarize yourself with the institution and the faculty. Review the faculty, memorize their names, and know a little bit about them. Who does what kind of research? Where did they get their degrees? Who might you know as a mutual friend? Bringing up these topics during an interview is very effective.

Major questions that you should ask several times of different people include, What is the mission of your institution? Is it changing? What do you believe the mission will be 10 years from now? If the mission of the university has been teaching and the institution is clearly trying to emulate a research university, this is important to know. The rules for success could change, and only those who understand and buy into these new rules will succeed.[11]

You have to know what the faculty and administration expect of you. And the differences can be significant. The 1990 Carnegie Foundation for the Advancement of Teaching study found, for example, that at research universities, the most important indicators for tenure or promotion are, in order of importance:[12]

1. Number of publications
2. Caliber of the journals in which the publications appear
3. Recommendations from outside scholars

At teaching institutions, on the other hand, the three most important indicators for tenure and promotion are:

1. Student evaluations of teaching
2. Service to the university community and the public
3. Number of publications

Often universities and colleges, in their public statements, claim that the three responsibilities of the faculty are to do teaching, scholarship, and service. The ugly sister of this trio is service. First, different universities define service in different ways. At most private universities and colleges service means internal committee and administrative effort—serving on the curriculum review committee, for example. At many public universities, especially the land grant institutions, service means serving the people of the state through continuing education or extension programs. In most public schools of education, for example, the faculty are expected to devote some fraction of their time *pro bono* to the local schools.

Is service, however it is defined, really as important in tenure decisions as universities claim? Yes, if service is required in such institutions as land grant colleges. No, if the university has a record of granting tenure based exclusively on scholarship. At such universities, it is perfectly safe to ignore the service requirement and concentrate only on scholarship. Enlightened departmental chairs will shield young faculty from committee assignments, recognizing that for them the time spent on service is time wasted.

Workloads also vary according to the mission of the school. The Carnegie report notes that at research universities, professors spend about 8 hours per week preparing for teaching, while those at teaching institutions spend 13 hours per week. At research institutions, professors spend 22 hours doing research and scholarship, compared with only 9 hours in teaching institutions. The type of teaching also differs. At large teaching institutions, the average size of the class is 29, compared with 82 students in large introductory classes at research institutions.

One of the staples of your conversations with the faculty will be one-on-one sessions. These commonly last 30 minutes, and you will find yourself telling the same stories many times over. During the interviews, you should also ask questions of your hosts. Ask about *their* research. Ask about the students and the facilities. Be inquisitive. Most important, be enthusiastic. The host faculty want to believe that you are just dying to come to their university. It's kind of like rushing for a fraternity or sorority. The faculty (fraternity brothers and sorority sisters) value your enthusiasm because it confirms the wisdom of their own decision to accept the bid to join the department (fraternity or sorority).

One question you might ask involves teaching. Often, courses in the undergraduate program become proprietary. That is, a course might be taught by the same faculty member for many years, and this person would take it as a personal threat if someone else expressed an interest in teaching this course. Generally, the faculty are interested in how your teaching interests might fit into the standard scheme. If you are replacing a faculty member, most likely you will teach the courses left vacant. But often there are no clear indications of what you are to teach. Your response should show that you have given this some thought and that you are confident that you can teach the course. But avoid overconfidence. Do not advertise yourself as being able to teach every course in the catalog.

The actual questions you will be asked during an interview will be as diverse as the interviewers. There are some classics, however, which fall into the categories of research, teaching, school activities, and career aspirations.[13]

Research. Describe you dissertation research. How is this a significant contribution to the field? Why did you choose this topic? If you were to begin it again, are there any changes you would make in your dissertation? What are your plans for applying for external funding?

Teaching. What classes are you now teaching or have taught recently? How would you structure teaching a class in your first semester? How would you encourage students to major in our field?

Participation in school activities. How, and what, can you contribute to our faculty? How much are you willing to participate on university committees and extracurricular activities? In what ways and in what areas do you see yourself making professional contributions in the next 5 years?

Self-image/Career choices. Tell us about yourself. (Memorize a concise, 1- or 2-minute summary of your background.) What are your strengths and weaknesses? (Respond by admitting to a "weakness" that is honest but would not be something that would be a major negative attribute in performing the job.) How do you spend your leisure time?

Try not to argue with the interviewer, but also do not be intimidated. Some interviewers believe that their job is to challenge candidates to see how they behave under pressure. Be firm and nonargumentative.

Do not volunteer negative information. Be positive about your experience and skills. Imagine the impression created by a candidate volunteering information such as, "I really did not like teaching this course. I don't think I was right for it," or "My research is certainly interesting to me but I don't see a great deal of reaction from the discipline to my ideas," or "Well, of course I put the best reviews of my book in the dossier. You should have seen some of the less complimentary ones!"

Experience in teaching undergraduate courses is very useful if the job entails such responsibilities. Be prepared to talk articulately about the structure or philosophy of courses you have taught and how you approached the learning experience. Be sure you have some ideas about how to improve such courses and/or how to apply the lessons learned to the teaching of other undergraduate courses. Showing how your research or scholarly interests relate to the courses can be very valuable.

Sometimes, if you are lucky, you will have a chance to talk to the graduate students without faculty present. This is always a good chance to ask tough questions. Graduate students are your kin, of course. You are one of them. They see themselves in your position in the not too distant future and will be honest with you. Ask about teaching loads, faculty and student morale, funding, departmental decision making, and so on.

During your talk with the department chair and the dean (and perhaps the provost)—that is, the people who will be your administrative superiors—the interview will be more formal. You should be aware that in such interviews, certain questions are considered out of bounds. Questions that may lead to illegal discrimination on the basis of race, sex, religion, national origin, or physical disability are prohibited—for example, "Are you married?" "What language did you first learn to speak?" "How many children do you have?" or "Have you ever run in a marathon?"

These questions are illegal because your answers might result in your being discriminated against on the basis of characteristics that have little to do with your job, although how these relate to possible discrimination for professors is unclear. The law assumes the worst possible situation and the most prejudiced of interviewers. In theory, if the interviewer has deep prejudice against Greeks, for example, admitting that this was your first language might lead the interviewer to grade you lower. The question about being married could lead to problems in relocating your spouse or prevent you from being on the road a lot. For sales positions when the customers are mostly Turkish, the married Greek probably would not have much of a competitive edge. But we are talking here about faculty positions. Most professors who will be interviewing you will not have the faintest notion that these questions are illegal. They will be interested to know if a spouse is involved because "two-body-problems" may require special handling. The number of children or what language your parents speak is simply irrelevant to your job, and speaking about them to your colleagues-to-be would be nothing but friendly banter. In the area of illegal questions, I would certainly give the interviewer the benefit of the doubt. Most faculty are actively and deeply committed to eliminating prejudice and bias on the basis of race, creed, color, or national origin and would not use your answers to discriminate unfairly in the hiring process.

Regardless of personal bias, however, cultural differences can come into play in the interviewing process in terms of expectations. If you are a foreign national seeking a job in the United States, you must realize that the interviewers will be either native Americans or fully American-ized permanent residents. As such, they will expect certain behavior from you, such as the willingness to shake hands and to preserve eye contact during the discussions. In some societies, such behavior is poor manners, and yet you will have to play the game by American rules. Foreign nationals can greatly benefit from staging mock interviews with other graduate students or faculty and videotaping these, and going over the important actions such as body language, voice volume, and eye contact.

Sometimes the toughest part of the interview, especially in front of a committee, is when you are asked for a 60-second synopsis of your dissertation. You have just spent a better part of a decade researching and writing this, and now you have to boil it down to a few words. Practice this in advance, because you will need it many times. Recognize also that you are speaking to people who may not be familiar with the topic. Be prepared to respond to questions based on ignorance of the field.

The Seminar

You have survived the interviews, and now it is time for the seminar. What are the faculty looking for in the seminar? Why do they make all applicants go through this rite of passage?

They are looking for two things: They want to know what research you consider important and how you can present the material. In the first case, this is an opportunity for you to tell them what *you* believe to be exciting in the field. Make sure it is substantive. Get down into the nitty-gritty of the material. The seminar should be an illustration of your scholarly capabilities, not a classroom lecture.

The second thing the faculty are looking for in your seminar is how you make the presentation, regardless of the content. Do you bring enthusiasm to the topic? Can you make a good oral presentation? Can you organize a seminar to make it interesting to others? Do you know how to use visual aids? And possibly most important: How do you respond to questions? Do you belittle the questioner or blow off the question? Or do you enter into a dialogue that shows your willingness and interest in collaborating with others? Can you handle the tough questions? If challenged, can you defend yourself?

Do not start your talk with a slide that shows your outline. This is boring and a waste of time. Start with something interesting that introduces your theme. Remember that the first few sentences are the most important part of your talk. Don't squander them.

In preparing visuals, make them specific to the location and date of the talk. Do not use the old ones from a conference you recently attended if the conference name is on the visuals. Here the advantage of using computer-aided visuals is apparent, since these details can be readily changed.

After the seminar, you might go out to dinner with the search committee or a select group of faculty or you might attend some other social affair. Do not forget that even though your seminar is over, you are still on display, so do not make a fool of yourself by telling off-color jokes or drinking too much.

The Second Visit

In some universities, after the initial round of visits, the prime candidate is asked to come back for a second visit and is often asked to bring his or her spouse to look over the area. At this point in the search process, the tables are turned. The university has decided it wants to hire you, and you are in a position of power. You can say "no," and the committee members will have to rethink their strategy, or even reopen the search—a huge pain and expense. They want to hire you. Talk to them about start-up funding and lab space and teaching assistants and rank and moving expenses and salary. Do not be bashful. Tell them what you want. You might actually get it.

The second interview is also your opportunity to ask some hard questions about tenure and promotion. Ask for facts, not opinions. It makes little sense to ask "Is tenure difficult to obtain?" Instead ask "How many assistant professors have been hired during the last 10 years and what has happened to them?" If some assistant professors tried to obtain tenure and were not successful, ask why and how they failed. Did the department not recommend them for tenure? Were they turned down at the university level? You should also ask how many other junior faculty members would come up for tenure with you. It also does not hurt to ask what standards are commonly required for achieving tenure, even though you will get widely different responses, simply because tenure is seldom based on numbers of publications, grants, or students but is a reflection of your quality and promise.

This is also the time to settle on your start-up funding (your "dowry"). In the natural sciences and engineering, start-up funding is absolutely necessary, and you should expect a significant offer if you explain why you need the funds. Start-up funds in the range of $250,000 are not unheard of at major research universities. At smaller comprehensive universities, the amount would be much smaller, although if you make a case for a major piece of equipment, you will probably get it. The dean wants you to hit the ground running and not waste time in getting your own external funding, and the dean expects this investment to be paid back in overhead funds in the near future. At the very least, even for humanities faculty, the least you should expect is a new computer for your office.

If you are a "two-body problem" with a spouse who will also need a job, then you have an additional degree of complexity in your job search. This is most acute when your spouse is also (as is so often the case) a person who seeks an academic career. How do you manage this complication in your job search?

First, figure out what exactly you are willing to accept. Will it be absolutely necessary for your spouse to have a tenure-track job at the university? Will he or she be willing to work part-time? Will a professional job with the local industry be acceptable or even desirable? Once you have decided on your strategy, you need to let your recommenders know. Often they will be called by the search committee to sound out what options they believe you will be willing to entertain. Asking you directly can be construed as illegal, of course, so the information must come from a circuitous path. Your recommenders need to know exactly how to respond to these questions, so you have to make sure they are aware of your decisions.

There is no need to volunteer this information to the search committee in your letter of application. When they express interest in you and invite you for an interview, you should be prepared to tell them about the complication if asked, as well as explain what you have decided is either necessary or desirable.

For foreign nationals, the job search is somewhat more complicated and, quite honestly, much more difficult. If you are interested in only a one-year appointment, your visa will allow you to stay for "practical training" following graduation, and you should not apply for tenure-track appointments. If a department hires you, it has to help you obtain a "green card"—work permission beyond the first year. Your specialized training will make it fairly easy to argue that you are unique and are not taking the place of an American citizen. All universities have special offices that deal with this paperwork, but the amount of time is substantial and the effort is difficult. Retaining a good immigration lawyer, even with the help the university gives you, is highly recommended.

In any case, one of the most important rules is to keep your recommenders apprised of your progress. Having one of them be blind-sided by a telephone call from an old buddy at the prospective university will not help your case.

The Rejection

Maybe, after all your hard work, you do not get "the offer" and are left holding the proverbial bag. Unemployed.

Hara-kiri?

Not quite. There may be many reasons why you have not succeeded this time around. Assuming an unbiased and totally fair system of matching people to jobs, it could mean that you are simply not right for the institution. Remember that there are 3,699 more institutions of higher learning in the United States, and surely somewhere there will be a perfect match. If you are serious about an academic career, try, try, again.

In some fields (like modern languages, where the supply greatly exceeds the demand), students spend several years in job searches, often accepting part-time work in the meantime.

A deeper reason for not getting an offer is that the decision makers have decided that you are simply not cut out to be a professor, regardless of the institution. Your potential employers all see something about your background or interests or behavior or references that leads them to believe that you would not be happy and productive in an academic career. Maybe they are right.

But if you feel that the negative result is a clear signal that you should give up this quest, then you have to have a "Plan B." Plan B would be another way you could apply your hard-earned new skills in a profitable and interesting way. English majors are always in demand in journalism. Chemists can make a good living with pharmaceutical companies. Good technical writers are notoriously difficult to come by. Psychologists can fashion meaningful careers in social services. And on and on. Maybe you will find that the alternative career is in fact very rewarding and will someday look back at this rejection with pleasure. When things went wrong, my grandfather used to say "Who knows what it is good for."

The Offer

Perhaps all your hard work has paid off, and there really is "the offer." It usually comes from the provost or the dean, on heavy-weight paper designed to impress you. If this is your first choice, accept at once. Everyone will appreciate this. If you have other offers in the fire, however, tell them when you will make up your mind. Be honest if they ask where else you are being considered. Deans have even been known to sweeten the pot just to not have to go through another search.

Suppose you accept an offer, and a week later you get an offer for your "dream job." Can you in good conscience turn down the original offer? This is a tough call. You have a legitimate contract with the university, and they fully expect you to keep your promise. Turning them down can create hard feelings and may damage your professional reputation, at least at that university. They have by now probably informed all the other applicants that the position is filled, and it will be difficult for them to go back and convince their second choice that they are really their top pick and that they should come join their department. More than likely, the department will start the search all over again, a process that will cost them a great deal of time and money. On the other hand, if you have gone through the process in good faith and kept everyone involved informed of the state of your applications, then it will not be illegal or unethical to reject an offer already accepted in favor of a better opportunity.

  If you do get the offer and accept, you are on your way! Congratulations! Welcome aboard!

Notes

  1. *1995 Higher Education Directory.* Falls Church, VA: Higher Education.
  2. Gaff, J. G., & Lambert, L. M. (1996). Socializing future faculty to the values of undergraduate education. *Change* (July/August), 38-45.
  3. Gibson, G. W. (1992). *Good Start* (pp. 38-45). Bolton, MA: Anker.
  4. *Academe.* (1992, March-April). Washington, DC: American Association of University Professors.
  5. Some of the items for this list came from Heiberger, M. M., & Vick, J. M. (1995). *The Academic Job Search Handbook* (p. 171 as modified by Reis). Philadelphia: University of Pennsylvania Press.
  6. Accreditation agencies are semiautonomous organizations established to periodically review the curricula, faculty, and facilities of colleges and universities in order to determine if the programs are sufficiently rigorous and meet some minimum educational standards. In engineering, for example, the Accreditation Board for Engineering and Technology (ABET) visits each program at least every 6 years and recommends one of three alternatives: The program is to be fully accredited, the program is to show cause why it should not lose accreditation, or accreditation is withdrawn. Losing accreditation is very serious for a college or university, and most institutions will do whatever is necessary to please the accreditation board.
  7. Overhead is the indirect costs the university receives from each research grant, ranging from about 40% of the cost of the project to over 80%, depending on how clever the university has been in convincing the federal government in its cost of supporting the research. Overhead legitimately goes to pay for such items as the buildings, power and water, administration, support staff, and other costs.
  8. This is also true, incidentally, for serious scholars receiving "career awards." Those who receive them continue to receive them because the judges believe that the previous judges must have seen something worthwhile to reward.
  9. Reis, R. M. (1997). *Tomorrow's professor: Preparing for academic careers in science and engineering* (p. 159). New York: IEEE.
  10. Heiberger, M. M., & Vick, J. M. (1992). *The academic job search handbook* (p. 35). Philadelphia: University of Pennsylvania Press.

11. Such a shift in priorities occurred right after World War II, when some universities changed from primarily undergraduate institutions to research universities almost overnight. Suddenly faculty who were hired to teach undergraduates were expected to do research and secure external funding. Many older faculty did not or could not do research and retired with hard feelings, believing that the university had reneged on the contract that emphasized teaching.

12. Carnegie Foundation for the Advancement of Teaching. (1990). *Identifiable comparable institutions.* Washington, DC: John Minter Associates.

13. Heiberger and Vick, *ibid.*

Appendix: Internet Resources

Internet Resources for Academic Job Hunting

Academic Employment Network: http://www.academploy.com
Academic Position Network: http://www.apnjobs.com
The Chronicle of Higher Education: http://www.chronicle.merit.edu
American Anthropological Association: http://www.ameranthassn.org/carplc.htm
American Philological Association: http://shemesh.scholar.emory.edu/scripts/APA/APACLASSICS.html
Modern Language Association: http://www.mla.org/main_jil.htm
American Mathematical Society: http://www.ams.org/employment
American Astronomical Society: http://www.aas.org
American Chemical Society: http://www.acs.org
American Physics Society: http://www.aps.org/jobs/index.html
Geological Society of America: http://www.geosociety.org/index.html
American Association for the Advancement of Science: http://www.nextwave.org
American Political Science Association: http://www.apsanet.org
American Sociological Association: http://www.asanet.org

CHAPTER 3

Learning to Teach

For many years, educators believed that the learning process was one of writing useful information on a blank slate in a student's mind—the *tabula rasa* theory. Effective teaching simply employed the most efficient transfer of this information.

Modern educational theory has pretty much debunked this notion. Students do not just receive information; they also *construct* knowledge in their minds, basing it on what is already there, and using the new information to make connections and create new concepts. The objective of teaching is therefore to help students learn. This concept has revolutionized the teaching profession, particularly at the K through 12 level. Universities have been much slower to change traditional teaching techniques.

In this chapter, I first discuss how students learn, what motivates students, and how we can help in their intellectual development. Based on these ideas, a course is constructed. In subsequent chapters, I describe the different instructional techniques such as lectures, seminars, and laboratories.

How Students Learn

Traditional teaching methodology has concentrated on the delivery system, not on the learners. A lecture, after all, can occur whether or not there is an audience. But effective teaching requires *learning,* and thus the student has to be brought into the process. Teaching must involve the rearrangement and development of students' preconceived notions and ideas, and this work has to be done by the learners. The teacher can provide opportunities for such rearrangement to take place.

Learning requires the student to take what is familiar, rearrange it in new cognitive structures, and produce new understanding. This process is obviously a spiral. A question is asked. How does something work? Is there another way of looking at this concept? How can we solve the problem? What happens if we do this or that? Next, the relevant facts are stated and/or terms are invented to describe certain things. Using these facts and terms, new ideas are developed and new theories are constructed. Understanding happens, often through discussions with others in laboratory and homework study groups. The new understanding suggests other questions ("So if this is true, then what would happen if . . .") and the process starts all over again. This process resembles a spiral where new concepts are always built on prior ideas that have been given names and have been found to be useful for solving problems. This learning theory is called *constuctivism,* and it differs markedly from two earlier theories, *behaviorism* and *maturationism.* The behaviorist learning theory is based on the notion that everything we know comes to us as a result of outside stimuli. If we do not learn the alphabet, we get rapped across the knuckles and then we learn it. Pain (and of course pleasure) stimulates learning. Maturationist notions of learning assume that humans are incapable of learning something until the mind and body are able to cope with the new thought. On hindsight, both concepts are clearly inferior to the constructionist theory of learning.

Consider an example that illustrates the idea of constructive learning (see Figure 3.1).

Figure 3.1. The Classic Lantern Problem

You might remember this puzzle from when you were a kid and your parents wanted to keep you busy on long car trips. Draw the lantern without lifting your pencil off the paper and without going over any line more than once.

You might have puzzled with the geometry, finally recognizing that you could cross lines and can think of the entire lantern instead of dwelling on each single geometric shape. You were presented with a problem, and you constructed a new idea—crossing lines to draw the figure.

But now let's make the puzzle a little more difficult. Suppose we again want to draw the lantern with a single pencil stroke and without traversing any line more than once, but now we want to start and end at the same place. Try it.

So why can't you do it? What is it about this simple lantern that prevents you from solving the problem? Here comes the extension of the existing knowledge. Can the idea be boiled down to some principles that would apply to such routing? In a class, the instructor might assign this as a group problem, and wait for the answers to evolve through logical deduction.

This is, in fact, precisely the problem presented in 1736 to the famous Swiss mathematician Leonard Euler (1707-1783). He was the court mathematician in Köningsberg (now Kaliningrad) and was supposed to solve problems for the king. One day the king wanted to have a parade, and the route of the parade was to be such that it would cross each bridge over the River Pregel only once and would return to its starting place. Euler's problem is pictured in Figure 3.2:

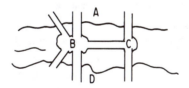

Figure 3.2. The Bridges of Köningsberg

Not only did Euler show that such a route was impossible for the king's parade, but he generalized the problem by specifying what conditions are necessary to establish such a route, now known as a *Euler's tour.* Euler noted that travel takes place along specific links (streets and bridges in Euler's problem) that connect nodes (intersections). A Euler's tour is possible only if the number of links entering all of the nodes is even numbered. The nodes in Figure 3.3 all have an odd number of links, so the parade the king wanted was not possible.

Similarly, the lantern problem is impossible to solve because the links at two of the nodes are odd-numbered (see Figure 3.4).

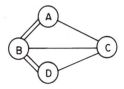

Figure 3.3. The Bridges of Köningsberg Reduced to Nodes and Links

Figure 3.4. The Lantern Reduced to Nodes and Links

So what have we done? We started with the familiar—the lantern problem. We asked a question: What would happen if we wanted to start and end at the same place? We gave names to parts of the problem—nodes and links—and we (Euler) discovered that there is a general concept here. We now know more than we had known before. We had a cursory understanding of networks that can now be applied to many other concepts such as electric circuitry and the routing of solid waste collection vehicles.

In summary, start with the familiar, ask questions, build on what students know, give it names, analyze and generalize, and then propose theories and conclusions which should in turn present new questions.

Sensory Learning

Now we turn to how the information the student uses can best be presented so that the student can start the construction-of-new-knowledge process. Obviously, this has to be through the senses. We have to hear it, see it, smell it, taste it, or touch it. The following are some examples.

- Anyone who has taken organic chemistry will agree that one's olfactory sense is important in learning. There indeed is a "ketone smell," and you can then group these organic chemicals into a single family.
- Cooking classes would be of little use unless the students tasted their products.
- Walking around the Gettysburg battlefield and identifying the locations of the troop units during the battle gives a far greater sense of history than just reading about the Battle of Gettysburg.
- Touch can be useful in illustrating the practical side of theoretical problems. In concrete design class, for example, having to handle a Number 4 reinforcing bar is instructive. One gets a clear sense of the mass and strength of this piece of steel. When problems are solved in which the number of such bars is the question, one can *feel* their presence in the concrete.
- Static water pressure becomes real when a large plastic liner is placed in a 55-gallon drum and the drum filled with water. Try inserting your arm between the plastic liner and the drum and push out. Wow! Now you understand static water pressure.
- Henry David Thoreau should be read only while sitting under a tree in a forest. The ambiance of the place provides much help in understanding his writings.

Although taste, smell, and feel are important learning senses, the two that are most used by students learning new material are sight and sound.

Visual learning occurs through graphs, pictures, diagrams, figures, images, and other graphical devices. Some students do not understand the concept of a hydraulic jump, for example, until they have *seen* one. Otherwise it is not real. They like to see mathematical functions plotted. For example, the equation $Y = 1 - 2X$ has little meaning until it is plotted (see Figure 3.5). Then the function has meaning. The student can then *see* the mathematical equation.

Auditory learning is the most common learning for university students. Unfortunately, this appears to also be the least efficient learning method, as discussed in Chapter 5.

Different disciplines tend to vary in how the majority of the students learn. Engineers, for example, tend to appreciate visual learning, while humanities students tend to be better auditory learners. Perhaps this is

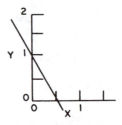

Figure 3.5. Picture of Y = 1 – 2 X

self-selection, in that students who learn by visual means tend to migrate to fields where visualization is most important.

Motivation

But when all is said and done, the construction of the new material has to be by the student, and the student has to expend the energy to learn the material. What EXACTLY is the motivation to learn? Why do some students learn so much better and faster than others?

Many years ago Maslow, a psychologist studying the question of human motivation, suggested that there is a hierarchy of human needs, as illustrated in Figure 3.6.

Maslow argues that the most basic human needs are the physiological needs such as food, water, air, and shelter. Only when these needs are met will humans seek the safety needs such as security, freedom and order. Likewise, if safety needs are met, humans will seek belongingness and love needs, then esteem needs, and finally cognitive and aesthetic needs. Finally, Maslow defined something called *self-actualization,* becoming what we are most fitted for, when the other needs are met and we can "be all we can be."

What are students' needs? First we must acknowledge that students are different and that they have different needs. Consider a student from an intellectually disadvantaged background who has worked hard but never quite overcome the nagging feeling that he or she is not quite as "good" as everyone else. One major setback, such as a poor course grade or rejection of an application, can be devastating and have long-term

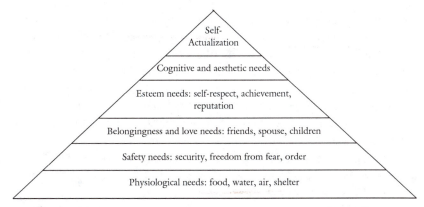

Figure 3.6. Maslow's hierarchy of needs.[1]

consequences. Ideally, the professor must recognize significant gender and cultural differences and design the learning experience to respond to the individual needs. Practically, this is impossible in large, impersonal classes.

At the very least, we hope that basic physiological needs of our students are met,[2] that students feel safe, that they are socially adjusted, and that they have friends. It seems to me that we professors are then working on the next level of student need—the self-esteem level. Learning things is fun. Learning things makes life exciting. Learning things makes more sense of the world. Learning things makes it possible to do things that were impossible to do before. Learning things results in new insights on the human condition. Why are we here, anyway, and what is the future of the human race? It is exciting to come closer to answering these questions, and this knowledge moves us ever higher on Maslow's scale. And perhaps, with all this education, we could eventually reach "self-actualization." Our job as professors is to make that possibility seem like a worthwhile option for our students.

Intellectual Development

Beginning with the pioneering work of Jean Piaget on the moral development of children, followed by Lawrence Kohlberg's longitudinal studies on how young men develop their moral reasoning, there has been a wide appreciation of the fact that young people continue to mature in their moral as well as cognitive complexity.[3] Little children, for example, have little sense of moral values and are entirely dependent on their parents. Slowly they begin to realize the concept of authority, then discover that their interactions with other children can result in various rewards or penalties. They begin to sense that they are individuals in a society and that this society has rules. Following the rules often results in personal benefits. Eventually, young adults recognize that there are good rules and bad rules, that some rules ought not to be obeyed, and that there may be universal moral values.

Carol Gilligan, while recognizing that there is such development, pointed out that the form of moral development for girls tends to differ from the way boys develop.[4] Values such as caring and helping are much higher on the scale of moral obligations for girls, while boys tend to place justice and fairness as the highest values.

William Perry has noted that cognitive development also occurs during the college years. He suggested that the progression of this cognitive development during college follows three steps[5]:

1. Dualism
2. Relativism
3. Commitment

In the first year of college, the student sees the world in absolutes— true or false, right or wrong, up or down—or *dualism*. There are simple answers to everything, and the student is sure he or she knows what these answers are. They cannot tolerate such answers as "it depends" or "well, what do *you* think?"

In many ways, we professors encourage such an outlook. Freshmen take introductory courses in which there are right answers. The sum of the forces around a point is *always* zero. Ayn Rand's ethical egoism *is* the best personal philosophy. Kirchoff's rules *always* apply. George Washington *was* the first president of the United States. The world *is* deterministic, and most important, the professor *is* the authority.

But through a maturation of outlook (and no doubt a lot of late-night bull sessions) the dualistic facade begins to crack. Sometimes professors, the omnipotent authorities, do not agree. They actually argue with each other. What, then, can be right? Maybe nothing is right. Perhaps all answers are just as good as any other answers. It probably really *does* depend.

Professors have a critical role to play in such development. During the first year, they must recognize the level of learning maturity of the students, but, at the same time, they must challenge students and encourage them to move on to the necessary second stage. Professors must also recognize that this is a transient stage; with help, students will continue to mature.

Sophomores characteristically wallow in *relativism*. This is the breaking out stage: breaking out from their preconceived dualist notions of the world and breaking out from the influence of their upbringing. Parents suddenly might not have the right political leanings. Maybe Marx had it right after all. Maybe if I wear scruffy clothes and grow a beard (or pierce my body, or get a tattoo) I will find some meaning in all this meaningless universe.

Sometime in the junior year comes a stage of self-discovery, a commitment to some issues or principles. Students find out that, although there may not be right answers, there may be many answers, and some answers are clearly better than others. Maybe Marx did not have it right after all. All the knowledge learned begins to take on context with the rest of the world. Students are no longer visitors on this planet but members of a community. They begin to see themselves as preprofessionals and take part in student professional societies.

Knowledge of such development is useful because the teacher (professor) has to be aware of students' stages of development and teach at that level. It is counterproductive to teach a course at the freshman level, for example, that requires students to have a sense of belonging to the greater world. This is not what they are about. First-year students need answers—direct, nonambiguous answers.[6] Eventually they will begin to realize that this is not the way the world works, but during their freshman year, at that point in their cognitive development, that is what they are capable of assimilating. Similarly, teaching juniors and seniors at a dualistic level is criminal. Older students need to be challenged and prodded and stimulated with real problems that may not have ready solutions. At this stage of their development, they are capable of and indeed demand this type of instruction.

If all this stuff is new to you, do not feel alone. It is the rare Ph.D. program that includes instruction on teaching. And this is not a problem with the modern university. As Cornford observed in 1908, in a wry guide to young faculty on the politics of the university, "A lecturer is a sound scholar, who is chosen to teach on the grounds that he was once able to learn."[7] But most of you will be hired on the assumption that you know how to teach. Go figure.

Notes

1. Maslow, A. (1979). *Motivation and personality* (2nd ed.). New York: Harper & Row.

2. It may not always be a safe assumption. I once had a special visiting student from China who had a bad toothache and did not tell anyone for months because he did not have the money to go to a dentist and did not want to ask anyone for help. I found out about it only long after he had returned to China.

3. Kohlberg, L. (1981). *Essays on moral development.* San Francisco: Harper & Row.

4. Gilligan, C. (1982). *In a different voice: Psychological theory and women's development.* Cambridge, MA: Harvard University Press.

5. Perry, W. Jr. (1970). *Forms of intellectual and ethical development in the college years: A scheme.* New York: Holt, Rinehart & Winston.

6. I once gave a quiz to a freshman class in which I gave them much more information than they needed. I nearly had a riot on my hands. "What are we supposed to do with all this information? If you don't want us to use it, why did you give it to us? You are trying to trick us, aren't you?"

7. Cornford, F. M. (1908). *Microcosmographia academica: Being a guide for the young academic politician* (p. 11). London: Bowes & Bowes.

CHAPTER 4

Organizing a Course

Inexperienced instructors are often asked to teach a standard course with prescribed content, a standard text, and specified course structure. This leaves little room to organize a course that has your own trademark. Let us assume, however, that you are given nothing but a topic to teach, or better yet, you are given the freedom to develop your very own course from scratch. In this chapter, I discuss how you would approach organizing and designing such a course.

Deciding What Students Should Learn

How do you decide what topics to include in the course? Start by developing a *goal statement* for the course. At the end of the course, **what do you want students to be able to do?** Once you have figured out what your teaching goals are, then you simply have to design the course to make it possible for the students to know this material and be able to demonstrate those skills and processes that you consider important.

One way of deciding on course content is to divide the possible topics into four categories[1]:

1. Concepts
2. Skills
3. Processes
4. Attitudes

List the topics under these headings and from this list write the goal statement for the course. Include this statement at the top of your course syllabus.

Once you have decided on the goal statement, decide what experiences and assignments will help students develop these concepts, skills, processes, and attitudes. In other words, match your teaching methods to your goals.

For example, suppose you had to develop a course in environmental ethics. Let's list the contents under the four categories:

1. Concepts—basic approaches to environmental ethics, including anthropocentric, biocentric, and ecocentric ethical theories; use of classical normative ethical theories to explain attitudes toward nonhuman nature; environmental ethics in organized religion
2. Skills—compare and contrast the different approaches to environmental ethics; using rhetorical skills, defend one environmental ethic against another
3. Processes—use concepts of ecology to relate to environmental ethics
4. Attitudes—appreciate the complexity of the problem and yet recognize the urgent need to develop a workable environmental ethic

Based on this list, the goal statement might be the following:

At the conclusion of this course, using concepts from ecology, ethics, and religion, students will be able to describe, contrast, and appreciate the complexity of the various approaches used to develop an environmental ethic.

As an aside, make sure the tests given in the course match the goal statement. More on testing in Chapter 7.

In designing your course, identify the students you will be teaching. Will they be freshmen, or seniors, or graduate students, or a mix? Remember Perry's taxonomy discussed in Chapter 3 and develop the material according to what the students are capable of learning and ready to assimilate. Decide which reasoning skills you can teach freshmen, and do not give true and false tests to seniors.

Related to this, identify the level of cognitive understanding you want the student to achieve. Bloom, Englehart, Furst, Hill, and Krathwohl in 1956 observed that what professors teach can be classified according to such levels of understanding.[2] They described six such levels:

1. *Knowledge*. This is the lowest level of understanding, and consists of repeating verbatim facts and definitions. If you want students to memorize the value of π, then you ask them on the test what its value is. This is crude memorizing of facts and regurgitation of material memorized. The key word here might be *list* or *state*.

2. *Comprehension*. Students not only know the facts but can comprehend the meaning, like knowing the meaning of π. They should be able to paraphrase in their own words what this means in order to demonstrate an understanding of what it means. A key word here might be *explain*.

3. *Application*. Students can now apply an abstract idea to solve a problem. They should be able to use π to find the circumference of a circle. Obviously they have to know what the value of π is and then know what it means. In the application stage they can use it to get answers to problems. The key word here might be *solve* or *calculate*.

4. *Analysis*. At this stage. the student is able to break down difficult problems and solve them by understanding their interrelationships. To analyze something means to break it into smaller pieces that can be looked at in isolation. A key word here might be *derive*.

5. *Synthesis*. Putting all the pieces together again is synthesis. This involves creating something, or combining elements in a novel way. Engineers who design things are using this level of understanding. Freshmen and sophomores need help with such open-ended problems where there are no clear right answers. The key words might be *formulate* or *make up*.

6. *Evaluation*. Finally, the last level of understanding involves judgment. Is the solution logical? Does it make sense? Choose from among alternative answers and justify your choice. The key word here might be *select* or *determine*.

In order to design your course, you have to select the level of understanding you want your students to achieve, and this achievement must be measurable. Often you will mix things up and introduce some analysis, some synthesis, and some evaluation, but always state what it is you want the students to be able to do in the instructional objectives.

Next you have to select a variety of types of instruction you want to use. The classical method of instruction is, of course, a lecture, which is the most efficient form of teaching.[3] If you have to teach at the first three levels of Bloom's taxonomy (knowledge, comprehension, and application), then the lecture seems to be just as effective as other more time-intensive alternatives such as small-group seminars. However, as the level of understanding increases, there is an increasing need to engage students in discussion and give-and-take. Don't forget that students have to learn, and remember that their learning often comes from their own expressions of ideas. In summary, the higher the level of learning, the smaller the class must be and the more the student should be engaged. More on the presentation of a course in the next chapter.

Choosing a Text

You should have some idea of the text you will need. Most book publishers will be more than happy to send you a review copy of a text if they think you might adopt it for the class. Call them, and do not be bashful.

Do not be pressured by senior faculty into using a particular text just because this text has always been used by the previous instructors. Most courses are highly individualistic, and you should have the option to choose the text most comfortable for you. In some cases, of course, such as introductory physics courses, the text will be chosen by the faculty, and the same text will be used in all classes.

If you are choosing the text, you should also check on the price of the book(s). Some book prices, especially in engineering and the sciences, are outrageous. You should also know that the university bookstore often tacks on its own 20%. If the store cannot make a deal with the publisher, it buys the books at list prices and charges the student 120% of the price. A $90 book will cost $108 in the bookstore. Students will appreciate your concern about the high price of books.

There are many ways of using a text. You can go through a technical or scientific text page by page, assigning homework problems as they are presented in the book and lecturing on the material in each section in sequence, hoping that the author of the book has thought through the sequencing of the course materials. Or you can design your own sequence and hop around in the text if this is possible. Finally, you can use the book as a reader and present in class all the material students need. In the latter case, I strongly recommend that you write your notes using the same symbols that are used in the book. Students have a difficult time as it is with concepts; no need to make it more difficult by making them remember two symbolic codes.

In the humanities, textbooks are most often used for discussions and background for the lectures. If you are teaching a lower-level course (freshman or sophomore year), make sure you assign specific readings in the books. Do not expect students to read because they are interested. Tell them specifically what is to be read and what they are responsible for.

Finally, you can assign a textbook or books and simply put them on reserve in the library. This works well for small courses where the use of the books is intermittent. Do not, however, put your own beloved texts in the library. Books have legs.

An alternative to a textbook is a handout in the form of a coursepak. In very specialized courses this is almost a necessity because books might not even be available. In other courses currency is important and the students need to read stuff published only weeks ago. Coursepaks can be expensive, however, since the copy firms have to receive permission (and often pay royalties) to reproduce certain articles or chapters from books. Give the copy firm lots of time to get this done.

Writing the Syllabus

Make an outline or syllabus for the course. Linearity may be a difficult problem in science and technology courses. Students have to first know A before they can understand B. But A cannot be understood until they know C. Tragically, C cannot be understood until the student understands B. Where do you start?

Often there is no best way. Try it one way once. If it does not work, try it a second way. You will soon discover the least of the evils.

The course outline should contain these elements:

Course title and number. (Use the title given in the catalog and not the one you wished the course would have been called.)

Your name and how you can be reached. Specify your office hours. (Most colleges require a certain number of office hours. Check the faculty handbook.)

The times the course meets, including the laboratory sessions.

The rationale for the course, including the statement of instructional goals. Tell students what they will be able to do after taking this course.

The outline of lectures and laboratories and/or recitation sessions. There is disagreement as to whether a topic for every day should be listed or whether topics should be listed by weeks. My preference is for every day. You may fall behind, but then you will know you are behind. This will push you to catch up. Whatever you do, do not just leave a third of the course untaught because "we just ran out of time." **The syllabus is a contract with your students.** You should make every effort to teach what is on that document.

In extenuating circumstances, negotiate with the students. Tell them that you have overestimated the speed of instruction and that you cannot possibly cover all the material. Ask them what should be left out and explain the consequences. In effect, you would be negotiating a change order on the contract.

Some professors negotiate a contract with the students on the first day of class, passing out a proposed syllabus and asking for their input. One nice touch is to let the students vote on how the grades will be assigned. You might, for example, provide them with a form of Table 4.1 on the initial syllabus.

If students have a personal stake in learning the material they take it more seriously.

If at all possible, front-load a course by placing the major assignments at the beginning of the course instead of the end. Have as much work due as early as possible. If midterm grades are required, this will give you a basis for assigning those grades. Students who typically are required to write major papers and finish projects at the end of courses will be grateful for having your course front-loaded.

TABLE 4.1 Grade Statement on a Syllabus

Item	Proposed Percentage of Grade	Actual Percentage of Grade
Homework	25%	_____ %
Quizzes	25%	_____ %
Exams	40%	_____ %
Final exam	10%	_____ %

Assignments: Description of assignments and the dates they are due.

Grading: Show how the grades will be calculated. More on grading in Chapter 7.

Late policy: Tell students whether you will accept late homework or reports and under what circumstances. I find that if I tell them I will subtract 5% per day for late papers, they appreciate knowing this, and may sometimes choose to take a 5% hit to be able to postpone finishing a report or other assignment due to other commitments. Above all, make the policy public and apply it unvaryingly.

Other information important to the student: For example, to avoid confusion, I always include on the syllabus my policy about working together on homework (I encourage it) so there is no misunderstanding. If students *must* complete one assignment in order to pass the course (such as an oral presentation) then this is also spelled out. Telling the students all this on the first day of class is not nearly as effective as writing it on the syllabus. The syllabus is, I repeat, a contract.

Notes

1. Thanks to Elizabeth Vesilind, director of the Middle Schools Program at the University of North Carolina School of Education.

2. Bloom, B. S., Englehart, M. D., Furst, E. J., Hill, W. H., & Krathwohl, D. R. (1956). Taxonomy of educational objectives: The classification of education objectives. *Handbook I: Cognitive domain.* New York: David McKay.

3. By *efficient,* I mean the least cost per course, not the amount of material learned.

CHAPTER 5

Presenting
a Course

There are many ways to build the scaffolding that helps your students construct what they learn. A major part of course organization is deciding what form of presentation you will use. In this chapter, I discuss the most widely used method of presentation—the lecture—and then present some alternatives to the lecture method of instruction.

Lecturing

The lecture method of instruction has received a lot of bad press lately. Some educators will somewhat haughtily proclaim "they don't lecture," leaving the impression that all those who do lecture are educational Neanderthals.

The lecture method of instruction should not be so readily committed to its grave. A great lecture can be as effective as any method of instruction, and, done well, can be a memorable experience. Ken Stunkel is an eloquent defender of the lecture:

> Authentic learning demands individual concentration and labor that cannot be shared with others. At its best, a lecture is a critical, structured, skillful, thoughtful discourse on questions and findings within a discipline, delivered by a person who knows what he or she is talking about. Virtually by definition, students are incapable on their own of exploring the topic at the same level. The reason is simple: A good teacher is an authority. He or she has more knowledge, experience, and insight into a subject than the student does. . . a professor unable to exhibit intellectual authority in the classroom has nothing to "profess"

and is in the wrong job . . . A responsible lecturer displays lucid exposition, cogent argument, and enthusiasm about the subject. A good lecture usually provides opportunities for student comment, questions, and sustains dialectical exchange. Discipline for the students consists in listening, remembering, tracking arguments, exercising judgment about note-taking, and thinking about what is said in light of assigned reading. Above all, an objective of such intellectual training is to strengthen attentiveness, without which we can accomplish nothing.[1]

We can enumerate the advantages of lecturing over other modes of instruction:

- *Efficiency.* The lecture method of instruction is cost-efficient: There are lots of students per one instructor.
- *Familiarity.* Students expect to hear a lecture.
- *Versatility and flexibility.* Lectures can be changed readily, even in mid-lecture, when you suddenly are aware you are dying.
- *Currency.* Lectures can be easily updated as new material becomes available.
- *Proximity.* Lectures provide a live contact between the student and the instructor.
- *Variability in speed.* The pace at which material is presented can vary depending on the student understanding.

There are also some serious disadvantages of the lecture method. Consider the following:

- *Teaching and learning are disconnected.* In the lecture, the audience is ignored. The teacher, especially in large lectures, has no idea whether the audience is learning.
- *Dated material.* There is the temptation not to update and to use the same old notes.
- *Murphy's Law.* Things will go wrong.
- *No improvement.* Seldom will there be improvement in a professor's lecture style. Professors who are not good lecturers will seldom take the trouble to improve, and there is little incentive for them to do so.
- *Boredom.* Everyone is bored.[2]

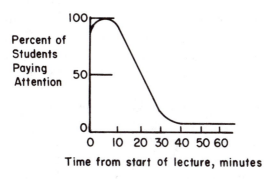

Figure 5.1. Typical Student Attentiveness Curve in Lectures

- *False efficiency.* It is not how many students you lecture to but how well students learn.
- *Energy expenditure.* It takes a lot of stress and energy to put on a good show.
- *Limited attention span.* Of all the problems with the lecture, the most important is limited attention span. Research has shown that the percentage of students in a typical classroom who are paying attention rapidly decreases after the first minutes of the lecture, as depicted in Figure 5.1.[3]

During the first few minutes of class, some of the students are still getting organized, and some are late in arriving. At about 10 minutes into the lecture, almost all of them are listening. But then the depressing depression. At 30 minutes, fully 85% of the audience is lost. (Most professors, of course, deny that this applies to *their* classes.) After 30 minutes, most of your students are no longer listening to you. At the end of a 75-minute lecture, you are talking to yourself. Research has shown that students retain about 70% of the material during the first 10 minutes of lecture, and only 20% of the material during the last 10 minutes of a lecture.

Outstanding lecturers will never let it get to such a low value but will plan their lectures in 20-minute segments, always doing something different at the end of each segment (giving a quiz, having a demonstration, getting students to form small-group discussion sections, etc.).

The quality of a lecture can be greatly enhanced by paying attention to some simple rules, the most important of which is the absolute necessity of *enthusiasm*. This is the single key to a good lecture. Make the students believe that you really like this stuff, that you find it fascinating, and that nothing would make you happier than to have the students share this enthusiasm. Without that enthusiasm, everything listed below is meaningless.

Here are some other pointers on giving good lectures:

Preparation. There is no substitute for it. Some of the most notable (and notorious) orators in history carefully orchestrated all of their speeches, practicing the delivery and listening to the sound of what they wanted to say. Adolf Hitler, for example, orchestrated all of his speeches, down to the minute gestures and eye movements. Only a few public figures, such as Abraham Lincoln, had the skill and stature to scribble a speech on the back of an envelope and have it become a historic document. Prepare your lectures by practicing in front of a mirror, or by videotaping yourself. These exercises can be ego-crushing, but they are well worth the effort by helping you become a poised and confident lecturer.

Timing. Always prepare the lecture to be too short. Once on your feet, time contracts. You will be amazed that the lecture you thought would take 30 minutes has stretched into 50 minutes.

Volume. Talk louder than you think you should. But also vary the pitch and volume of your voice. Remember that emphasis can be added by speaking louder or softer. Great choirs can have their audiences holding their collective breaths by whispering.

Fiddling. Leave your belongings alone. Do not jingle coins in your pocket, do not adjust your hair or your necktie, tug at your earring, click a ballpoint pen, check if your fly is up, and so forth.

Appearance. Look good. Do not overdress, but be neat. Remember that you are the most important visual aid in your lecture. You are what the students will be looking at, and proper appearance and effective body language are important elements of any presentation.

Motion. Stand still most of the time. Use movement for effect. If you want to emphasize a point, move in toward the audience, even leaning into the audience, and make sure everyone is looking at you, then whisper your message as if you are taking each and every one of them into strictest confidence.

Bearing. Do not droop or lounge over the podium. Stand tall.

Confidence. Never apologize. Never tell the students that you have not had the time to prepare . . ., or that you have a cold . . ., or that your slides are lousy . . . or whatever. If the slides are truly lousy, the students will know soon enough. There is no sense in emphasizing an already deplorable situation.

Humor. Be careful of jokes. A quick and dirty way to die in front of students is to tell a joke that is not funny to them.

Profanity. Do not use it.

Structure. Use acceptable grammar, and speak in complete sentences. Also finish your sentences. Some speakers will have so much information in their heads that they simply overwhelm themselves and start innumerable sentences, never finishing any. Words need to be in complete sentences in order to make sense.

Presence. Remember where you are. Everyone is looking at you and listening to you, so do not talk to yourself. Many speakers think out loud, such as "Let's see now, should I show this overhead now or later?" or "This is not straight on the projector," or "Where do I go from here?" Such musings are highly distracting and give the impression that you are making it all up as you go along.

Answering questions. The larger the lecture hall, the fewer will be the questions. Students are intimidated by large class size and will not want to risk appearing stupid in front of hundreds of their classmates.

Eliciting questions from students in lectures is difficult, but you can help by remembering some basic principles. Do not, for example, ask "yes or no" questions. Ask reflective questions like "What would you do in this situation?" or "Why do you suppose he acted in this way?" If there are no responses, try giving clues. "Well, let's think this through. He was a second-term president. Why would he have vetoed that bill?"

Give the students enough time to think of an answer. Do not spring the question on them and then two seconds later effectively withdraw it. Let them think at least 5 seconds. This is a very long time! Try timing some professors. Generally, they cannot stand dead air time and will jump in within 2 or 3 seconds.

Encourage students to put up their hands immediately if they have questions, but tell them that you will finish your thought and then call on them.

Most important, how you respond to students' questions or suggestions will determine the kind and number of responses you will receive from the students. If students perceive you as unfair, they will cease all dialogue. One survey of student attitudes found that fairness is very important and that they expect fairness in the classroom. Violation of this fairness was defined as "being angry or mean, . . . embarrassing students in the classroom, especially using sarcasm and put-downs, exhibiting an uncaring attitude toward students, and failing to respond to student questions."[4]

Getting the students involved. The more students participate in the lecture, the more they will stay awake and attentive, and the more they will learn. Student involvement is critical to learning, as pointed out by the National Institute of Education.[5] The fundamental principle is this:

> The amount of student learning and personal development associated with any educational program is directly proportional to the quality and quantity of student involvement in that program.

One way to get the students involved and to spice up your lecture is to present an "everyday ethical dilemma" and have students respond anonymously in a short paragraph. You would then collect these and discuss the answers the next day. These dilemmas would not have clear answers but would present a contemporary problem for reflection.[6]

The *one-minute paper* has been widely used with many variations. The classical one-minute paper requires you to finish the lecture a few minutes early and then ask students to write a short paper on the question "What was the most important thing you learned in this class?" or "What important question remains unanswered?" Collect these papers as the students leave the room. Looking over the papers you can get a quick sense of what the students learned, and if you believe that they missed an important part of the lecture, you can correct it the next time. Be sure to refer to these papers at the start of the next lecture to allow students to recognize that you have indeed read them and that you are taking their feedback into account. One-minute papers also provide a quick method of taking roll and identifying students who have multiple absences.

Alpha and omega. Have a good beginning and a good ending. In a public presentation, remember that your goal in the first few minutes of a lecture is to convince the audience that you are worth listening to. These first 2 minutes are when you have their undivided attention, so make the most of them. Be careful with the magical words "In summary . . ." or "In conclusion . . ." You will raise expectations that you may not wish to fulfill. Say those words only when indeed you are about to conclude the lecture.

Using Visual Aids

Visual aids can greatly enhance your lecture. Psychological studies have repeatedly shown that learning is enhanced if two or more senses are used simultaneously. About 35% of all the information we retain is visual, and only about 15% is verbal. But if the two are combined, the effect is synergistic. For proof, look at any advertisement on television. Very seldom will a significant word be spoken without it also being printed on the screen.

The types of visual aids vary widely, from material demonstrations, to overhead charts, to videos, to computer applications. The most important rule on visual aids is that they all must be a necessary part of the lecture. This is not an opportunity to display a scrapbook of neat-looking pictures.

Here are some more pointers in the use of visual aids in public presentations:

Subordinate. The lecture is not the visual aids. The lecture must stand by itself; the visuals simply make it better. A potential problem with using slides for your entire lecture is that if, for whatever the reason, your slides are misplaced or lost in the projection booth, your lecture may be a total disaster. If the slides are subordinate to your lecture, you can still wing it.

Use your visuals as needed, then remove them from the screen. When you are not using the visuals, you want the audience to focus on you and not the pictures. When using an overhead projector, turn the projector off or remove the transparency. With 2 × 2 slides, leave blank slots where you intend to talk without the illustrations.

Check. And recheck. Run through the slides or overhead transparencies before the lecture in order to make doubly sure they are in the correct order. An upside-down slide is upsetting to the speaker and distracting to the audience.

Enlarge. Make the writing or graphics on your visuals "too big." For overhead transparencies, a viewing distance of 8 feet requires letters to be at least ¼ inch high on the transparency, a viewing distance of 16 feet requires ½-inch-high letters, and a typical classroom with a viewing distance of 32 feet needs 1-inch-tall letters in order to be legible for the average person from the rear of the room. A good guideline for 2 × 2 slides is that the writing should be visible without magnification by holding the slide up to light.

Redraw. Be careful about using visuals made from printed material. Visual aids for public oral presentation should be different from figures used in publications because the audience does not have the time to understand detail as you move along in your talk. Illustrations used in oral presentations should be open, clear, simple, colorful, and big. The listener does not have time to scrutinize the figure in order to understand it so the figure must convey the argument quickly. Always use horizontal lettering, because the audience cannot turn the paper sideways to read the vertical words. Note the size and shape of the slide and the overhead fields. The field in 2 × 2 slides is rectangular whereas the overhead projector has a square area for projection. Prepare your illustrations accordingly.

In technical or scientific courses where a lot of derivations are involved, consider using the "incomplete transparency" technique (sometimes called the "guided note-taking" technique). You start by writing the notes for your presentation but leave off some critical items like the definitions of the variables or the curves from the line graphs. Photocopy these pages for the students and at the same time make overhead transparencies of these pages. During the lecture use a colored pen to fill in the missing part of the transparency as the students are filling in their notes. This method gives students time to think about what is going on instead of madly trying to keep up with your writing. You can cover twice the technical material in a course using this technique rather than simply writing it all on the board. And, in the end, the students will have a compete and accurate set of class notes.

There are two kinds of ink pens for overheads—water-soluble and permanent. The former are useful if you intend to use the overheads again, such as in courses using the "incomplete notes" technique. Permanent markers are usually more opaque and hence are clearer, but they will not come off with water, spit, or similar fluids. One author contends that vodka will easily remove permanent ink, but I cannot recommend this as the best use of vodka.[7]

Chalkboard technique, even in the age of computer projection equipment, is still important. Be careful not to erase too fast on the board. Leave the stuff up long enough for everyone to write it down. Use large letters and figures. If you are in a large auditorium, use large chalk. This can be purchased as "railroad chalk" and is highly effective for making fat lines that students can read from a distance.

Learn to use the technology. Murphy's law will prevail. The bulb in the projector will blow out, and at the worst time. Unless you have a video technician handy, it is your responsibility as the lecturer to troubleshoot problems with projection equipment. You should learn how all of the projectors turn on and off, how they are focused, and what to do when the bulb burns out. Learn to run the VCR. You don't want to look like a ninny, unable to do anything but wring your hands when something does not work. Your credibility and authority will be severely eroded if you have no idea how to run simple video devices.

Alternatives to Lectures

The teaching method most often used in place of the lecture is the small-group seminar. In this setting, the instructor does not do all the talking but, rather, facilitates the discussion. The objective is to get the students to talk to each other, to challenge each other, and to think out loud to each other, with the instructor only acting as the occasional referee and arbitrator.

Small-group discussions present a whole new set of problems for the instructor, however. One of the thorniest is that not all students are created equal in their willingness and ability to carry on conversations in such settings. Invariably, there will be at least one loudmouth and at least one recluse who will refuse to say anything. Sometimes the only way to handle the loudmouth is to take him or her aside privately and just discuss the problem. In all likelihood, that student will be grateful for your help. More difficult is to get the recluse to say anything. Threats of "grade depends on class participation" seldom work. Patience and understanding are the best alternatives.

Evaluating the contribution by students when the "grade depends on class participation" is of course purely subjective. Waiting until the end of the semester to make such an evaluation leaves one open to bias. Excellent contributions at the beginning of the semester are forgotten, and the grade often depends on the last few weeks of performance. The best method is to write notes on the performance of each student after each class.[8] These do not have to be extensive notes, but enough to jog the memory and to even out your grading of participation throughout the semester.

Other teaching strategies include debates in which students prepare arguments for two or more sides to an issue. Often the best technique is for the instructor to assign the sides so that students are arguing opposite sides to what they might naturally believe. Not only does this enhance skills in rhetorical arguments, but it may even create new insights into how others believe. Tolerance of opposing views should be an educational objective.

Another small-group technique related to debates is to use role-playing in class. This works especially well for policy questions on which good people on all sides disagree. Again, the most effective technique is to assign roles to students contrary to their beliefs.

Another alternative teaching method is to invite outside speakers to class. Sometimes a colleague from another department will be effective in reinforcing points you made. Anyone who has been a parent will attest to the fact that children do not listen to parents, but if another adult says the same thing, it is somehow more believable and relevant. Bringing in another voice will benefit both the students and you. From the students' point of view, the most extraordinary event would be if the two of you disagree and start to fight it out in class. Students who might have thought that all professors were infallible suddenly recognize that legitimate differences of opinion exist. These debates make for memorable class sessions.

Especially in smaller groups (but also in larger sections) *cooperative learning* is a popular alternative. In theory, we learn a lot more from each other than from the instructor, and cooperative learning simply facilitates such interaction. Cooperative learning can be achieved in informal small-group (three or four students) discussions at opportune points during a lecture. Or, cooperative learning can be used in a more formal arrangement such as assigning groups for doing homework together. When such formal cooperative learning groups are used, there is always the question of whether the students should be allowed to choose their own groups or whether the instructor should assign the groups. Some educators are especially sensitive to gender issues and suggest that one woman should never be assigned to a group with three men because of the possibility of male domination. Some even recommend segregation by gender and race.

I strongly oppose this, and I have talked with many students about the issue. I have never had students tell me they thought that groups should be assigned on the basis of gender or race. In fact, students appreciated the opportunity to work with fellow students with whom they might not have voluntarily formed working groups.

Finally, there is the question of time versus material covered. In most standard courses, the time (a semester) is constant and the material is variable. The grade is supposed to be an indication of the amount of material mastered by the student, and this is variable. But if we turn this around, the logic would be that there should be a certain amount of material all students should learn, and it should not make any difference how long it takes the student to learn it. In such a case, all students should receive an A grade for having mastered the material, and the time the course runs is variable. This concept is called *personalized instruction* (or *outcomes-based education* or *mastery learning*).

In some personalized instruction schemes, students learn in self-paced workbooks, with lectures serving as rewards for having mastered material. They take tests when they are ready, and they may take a test as many times as necessary. They move on to the next material only after having mastered the previous material. All students will then receive either an A grade or, if they give up, an F grade. In other personalized instruction schemes, the class is tested as a group, and the entire group must demonstrate mastery before they can move on. This puts great pressure on the brighter students to bring along the less swift. In any case, the use of personalized instruction is effective but, as you can imagine, extremely instructor-intensive. As a result, the technique has not caught on in colleges but is being increasingly adopted in K through 12 public schools. As students familiar with personalized instruction or mastery learning enter colleges, they may increasingly demand that such instruction be adopted on the university level as well.

Notes

1. Stunkel, K. R. (1998, June 26). The lecture: A powerful tool for intellectual liberation. *Chronicle of Higher Education,* p. A52.

2. There is the old story of the professor who dreamed he was giving a lecture, woke up, and found that he was.

3. Based on data reported by Hartley, J., & Davies, I. K. (1978). Note-taking: A critical review. *Programmed Learning and Educational Technology, 15,* 207-224.

4. Rodabaugh, Rita Cobb. (1996). Institutional commitment to fairness in college teaching. In Linc. Fisch (Ed.), *Ethical dimensions of college and university teaching: Understanding and honoring the special relationship between teachers and students* (New directions in teaching and learning, No. 66, Summer, p. 37). San Francisco: Jossey-Bass.

5. *Involvement in learning: Realizing the potential of American higher education.* (1984). Washington, DC: National Institute of Education.

6. Flusche, M. (1996). Assessment of student work. In L. M. Lambert, S. L. Tice, & P. H. Featherstone (Eds.), *University teaching: A guide for graduate students.* Syracuse, NY: Syracuse University Press.

7. Fiebelman, P. J. (1993). *A Ph.D. is not enough: A guide to survival in science.* Reading, MA: Addison-Wesley.

8. Smith, David (1996). The ethics of teaching. In L. Fisch (Ed.), *Ethical dimensions of college and university teaching: Understanding and honoring the special relationship between teachers and students* (New directions in teaching and learning, No. 66, Summer, p. 13). San Francisco: Jossey-Bass.

CHAPTER 6

Meeting Your First Class

Scared.

It's as if you did not know how to drive a car and your parents gave you the keys and said "go for it." It would be exhilarating, but you would be scared to death. In this chapter, I discuss some of the anxieties we all experience in meeting our first class. And no, the anxieties never leave completely, but they can be significantly reduced by preparation and experience.

First-Time Fears

First-time fears might be categorized as follows:

- How can I adopt an appropriate pace for the students, and at what level of difficulty should I present the material?
- How can I teach this material if I have been increasingly specialized? I know an awful lot about a narrow area and now I have to teach a broad range of material in my discipline.
- How can I establish an appropriate professional demeanor with the students? I am, after all, not too much older than they are. What will they call me?
- But I don't know all the answers. They are sure to ask me something I don't know. How embarrassing that will be![1]

If you have any or all of these fears, don't feel like the Lone Ranger. Welcome to the club.

But let's address them in turn:

You will soon know if you are going too fast or too slowly. Gauge the students' progress with quizzes. *Ask them*. Make them feel like you care. They will be brutally honest with you once they realize that you really do want to know.

Yes, you have been "specialized," but you will be amazed at what you do know in your field. If you feel uncomfortable with a topic, you have plenty of time to read and catch up on the latest developments. Most important, don't be a recluse. Meet regularly with your colleagues to share their approaches to the subject. Get involved in the intellectual life of your university. Sit in on a few courses.

Establishing an appropriate demeanor is totally up to you. You can be friendly with the students, but you must never forget that you are in a position of power with respect to them. You cannot be their pal. They will soon learn to respect you for your knowledge and adjust to your professional demeanor. Let them call you what they want to according to the tradition of the school. In some colleges, first names are common; in others, only last names with titles are used. They will soon find what is comfortable for them. In general, it is better to start out more formally and, if all goes well, move toward a less formal style.

No, you don't know all the answers. None of us does. Big deal. You will soon learn that one of the best responses to a difficult question is "I don't know. How can we find out?" Use the occasion as a *teachable moment,* a situation when you can model the attitude of inquiry and curiosity about your field—to demonstrate that all the knowledge was not given to us on stone tablets but had to be learned the hard way.

By admitting that you don't know something, students will respect you for your candor and honesty. Don't ever try to bluff them. They can smell it and you will be in deep trouble.

So much for your fears. Don't let them get you.

The First Class Session

Here is how to be less scared: Prepare your first class with care.

Try to be early to the class. No need to make a dramatic entrance one minute after the class starting time. As the students trickle in, engage them in conversation. Students in classes seldom know one another very well at the beginning of the semester, and the place will be fairly quiet.

When it is time to start, introduce yourself to the class and tell them a little about your background. If you have an interesting name, you might talk about your ethnic background or about where you grew up. Someone in class will be from that area, and you will immediately establish a rapport with that student and indirectly with the class.

In most cases, the students do not know each other, and you do not know the students. Mutually learning names is a great advantage to everyone and will create an esprit de corps that will make the educational experience more pleasant for everyone. One way of getting everyone involved is to have students interview each other for about 5 minutes, then have them introduce the students they have just interviewed. A variation of this technique, applicable to small classes, is to have students for the second class meeting bring a paper bag filled with five items that have meaning to them personally. Pair the students and have each person guess what these items mean to his or her partner. After the guessing game, have each student introduce the partner using the knowledge gained from the five items in the bag.

Such semi-silly exercises will also help you to learn student names— the single most important variable in student evaluations! Students want to be real people and not just anonymous numbers in class. To help you memorize the names before the first class, write down the student names on index cards and, as they introduce themselves or are introduced by their partners, write on the card some telling characteristic of the person that will help you to remember the name. This techniques works especially well for larger classes.

For smaller classes, consider using nameplates. Give students blank cardstocks and have them fold the cards longways and write their names on them. If the class is in a circle, everyone will be able to learn each other's name. After class, save the nameplates and use them for the next few sessions until everyone is known.

Distribute your class syllabus and go over it very carefully. Explain about the texts and whether they should purchase the books, or if you have texts on reserve in the library. Talk about the objectives of the course. What are you trying to accomplish? "At the conclusion of this course, students will be able to . . . "

Discuss the grading policy. Make sure they understand your late policy.

Depending on the class, you may or may not want to define what you mean by "good manners." I have found this is very effective for first-year students. Freshmen sometimes simply don't know what good manners in a classroom are. For example, you might tell them that you want them to be on time and that class starts when it is scheduled to start. You might tell them that they are *not* welcome to get up and leave in the middle of the class (except in emergencies, of course). I have found that students simply do not know that this is boorish behavior, but once it is pointed out to them, they gladly become civilized. You might also tell them that it is *not* acceptable to do crossword puzzles or homework in class or to read other material. Depending on your sensibilities, you might suggest that eating in class is also not good manners and is discouraged. My experience has been that students do not think badly of you for saying all this. They appreciate knowing what the parameters of good manners are.

Finally, you should talk about your intention to treat them as honorable ladies and gentlemen and to trust that they will not betray this confidence by being dishonorable. You should clearly say what the rules here are. Are they allowed or even encouraged to do homework together? How about reading each other's papers and offering critiques? Be specific.

Also, wave the stick. Make sure they know that you take the honor commitment seriously and will prosecute students who betray your trust in them.

When the preliminaries are over and you have made sure they have no questions, make good use of the rest of the period. Don't just dismiss them with nothing to hang on to. Do something substantive and assign some homework or other outside-of-class activity.

So don't be scared.

Yeah, like none of was scared when we started. But you will get over being scared. Your concern will settle down to a base-level anxiety—and that is a good thing. You should always and forever have a slight queasiness in your midsection before meeting a class. When you lose that anxiety, you are either dead or academically comatose and should retire.

Note

1. Turner, J. L., & Boise, R. (1989). Experiences of New Faculty. *Journal of Staff, Program, and Organizational Development, 51* (Summer).

CHAPTER 7

Testing
and Evaluation

An integral part of your career as professor is evaluating the work of other people. As a professor, you will be evaluating students' performance as well as evaluating colleagues for promotion and tenure and for hiring. You will be evaluating papers sent to you by journal editors. You will be evaluating research proposals. The list goes on. And yet, we are never taught the basics of how such evaluation is to take place. It is on-the-job training.

In this chapter, I first discuss some underlying theory of evaluation of students by testing and then turn the tables to discuss the evaluation of professors by students.

Validity and Reliability

The effectiveness of a test is evaluated on the basis of its *validity* and its *reliability*. Validity refers to how well the test samples knowledge or skills the students are expected to learn. For example, if an instructional objective is to teach the students to memorize the value of π, then a question that reads:

Write the value of π to three decimal places:_____

has high validity. On the other hand, if the instructional objective is to remember the value of π and the question is:

What is π used for?_____

the test has low validity, because it does not ask the student to respond to the instructional objective.

Similarly, if the instructional objective is to be able to use Schoenberg's twelve-tone system of composition, a question such as:

> To what do you attribute the lack of popularity of compositions written using the twelve-tone system of composition?

obviously has low validity. Students would call a test with low validity "unfair."

A common problem in humanities is the muddling of the factual response with the quality of the presentation. Some students know how to write well; others do not. If the quality of writing is included in determining the grade, this must be included in the instructional objectives. Otherwise, a paper that is poorly organized, has many misspelled words, and uses bad grammar but includes all of the essential facts should not receive a low grade.

The second necessary characteristic of tests is their reliability, or how well the test discriminates between students of different levels of knowledge. That is, will the test measure the true ability to fulfill the instructional objective? Multiple-choice tests have low reliability because luck often plays an important role, as does the ability to take poorly written multiple-choice examinations. True-and-false tests have even lower reliability, and because of this characteristic, they should never be used in university teaching. Ideally, a test should yield the same results time after time or, in science jargon, should have high *precision*.

Tests with the highest reliability are short-answer or short-essay tests where a single fact or explanation is required. Multiple-choice tests can have high reliability if the questions are carefully worded. In writing multiple-choice questions, the *stem,* which poses a problem or states a question, should be clear, compact, and positive. In writing the *response,* write the correct answer first, then using the same style and tone, write the incorrect responses. Avoid using "always" or "never" or "all" or "none." Use "none of the above" as a response for numerical problems requiring calculation.

If there are four choices in a multiple-choice test, people with no knowledge whatever of the material should have a 25% chance of getting the question right. A well-written question should elicit at least 50% correct responses. Trick questions would receive a response of less than 25% for the correct answer and should not be used.

The reliability of essay questions or mathematical problems depends a great deal on the way they are graded. Being fair in grading becomes difficult in the face of diverse responses. With numerical problems, a correct solution receives full credit, but an incorrect one should receive some credit, depending on how close the student came to solving the problem. Similarly, in essay tests there is no truly correct answer, but some answers clearly respond completely to the question and should receive full credit. In both cases, it is necessary, before grading begins, to write down the points that should be included in the response and then use these to attain consistency in grading. For example, suppose the question was:

Explain the process of eutrophication in lakes.

_____

we would want to see the student include the following facts:

1. Algae use energy from sunlight and nutrients from the water to reproduce.
2. Nutrients limit the growth of algae.
3. Phosphorus is the primary rate-limiting nutrient.

and so on. Even though the response is written in the student's own words, the facts or concepts should be there, and checking them off gives a semiquantitative basis for a grade.

Giving Tests

Tests are useful for many reasons. You may want to gauge how well the class is doing and so you give a short quiz. Or you want to motivate students to do outside reading and test them at every class meeting.

(Students hate it, but when the course is finished, they will tell you how effective the quiz was in making them do the reading.) Or you may use it as a learning tool. Quizzes can be given at odd moments in a lecture when you believe students ought to have grasped some central idea. You may, in fact, lead them through the solution to the correct answer (easy grading, that one!). Finally, you test to find out how well the students have mastered the material, so that you can assign a grade. I believe that the greatest value of tests is as a learning tool, and tests are only incidentally an evaluative tool.

The rule of thumb on test frequency is the more the better. This will prevent sad situations when a student might have had one very poor grade and all the rest good grades and ends up with a low evaluation because of a single bad grade. Most important, tests developed by professors typically have low test reliability. To counter this, give a lot of tests.

Review again Bloom's taxonomy. What do you want to test? Do you want students to be able to memorize things, or do you want them to be able to evaluate things, or something in between? Make sure you understand the level of testing before you begin writing the test.

In writing test questions, do not use tricks. Trick questions accomplish neither the learning nor the evaluation purposes for a test. It is fair, however, to put homework problems on a test just to see if the students actually did the homework.

There is little logic in having a time limit on an examination. The purpose of an examination should not be how *fast* the students can write or solve the problem, but how *well* they can do it. Write a test that you yourself can finish in 25% of the time available. If the students will have only one hour for the test, you should be able to complete the test in 15 minutes.[1]

Students with documented learning disabilities sometimes require more time to finish a test. You can handle this informally or use the central student service centers where students can take proctored tests. More on this in Chapter 8.

To give makeup tests or not to give make-up tests? Experience has shown that if you do give makeup tests, you will have an amazing number of grandmothers die during the midterm period. On the other hand, there are extenuating circumstances for medical reasons. Again, tell the students ahead of time what your policy is and stick to it.

Each university or school has its own honor system, and you should work within that system in proctoring examinations. In some schools, tests can be taken at any time and at any place, and students are on their honor to work without assistance and to stay within an allowable time limit. Other schools use nonproctored examinations with the professor coming by occasionally to answer questions. Most schools, however, require that all examinations be proctored. More on this in Chapter 12.

Instructors can often be put into problematic situations when students ask for special favors and present all manner of excuses for either missing or postponing an examination. My experience has been that personal excuses ("I had to go to a funeral") tend to be genuine, while nonpersonal ones ("My computer crashed") tend to be bogus. I would never question a death in the family or any other serious personal problem. But I do not know of too many dogs that eat homework.

In some disciplines, open-book examinations are common. Collaboration and outright cheating can easily occur in such examinations, and they should be used with caution. Take-home exams should be given only when students are tested on their skills in researching a topic, or when the time to finish the examination would be too long for in-class testing.

Do not use red ink to grade test papers or homework assignments. Think of the symbolism: blood, stop, warning, etc. Use any color but red if you want to encourage your students to do better.

Comments on papers and examinations differ in strength. A comment on an A paper is meaningless, while a comment on a C-minus paper is strong. Be much more careful with writing comments on papers and exams with low grades. Also be careful with how things are said. Students cannot read the comments with the same meaning as they were written and may misinterpret your intentions.

I have tried all kinds of tests and find that the best way is to give the exam to all students at the same time, give them plenty of time, make it difficult for them to cheat, and tell them at the beginning of the test that I expect them to act like honorable ladies and gentlemen and that they will deeply hurt my feelings if they cheat on the examination.

Finally, with all the test results and homework grades in, you have to assign a final grade. I strongly recommend that you do not curve the test scores. Tell the students, for example, that if their final grade is 90% or higher they will receive an A grade, and so on. Never increase the threshold. Design your course so that there is a reasonable distribution of grades. If everyone has over 90% you should tighten up your course next semester in order to have an acceptable distribution of grades, unless you are using the mastery learning technique, in which case everyone should either have a high grade or fail the course.

In summary, your grading should:

- Be accurate. Take off points reflecting the severity of the mistakes.
- Be clear. Explain and justify the reasons for low grades.
- Be fair. The same mistakes must result in similar loss of points for all.
- Be compassionate. There are extenuating circumstances that will require you to bend your rules. Do so without making a big thing of it and, most important, without broadcasting to others.
- Be open to the possibility of an error in your grading.
- Be explained at the start of the course.

Student Evaluations

In many colleges and universities, especially where teaching effectiveness is important and good teaching is supported, student evaluations play a central role in determining tenure, promotion, and pay raises. As you would expect, a great deal of research has gone into determining just how valid these ratings are. This is somewhat of a shell game, of course, because there is no "truth" against which to compare the ratings, and some faculty have dismissed the ratings as irrelevant.

An immense amount of research, however, strongly suggests that student evaluations are useful and valid indicators of teaching effectiveness.[2] Nevertheless, every few years there seems to be a dustup when someone writes a piece suggesting that student evaluations are not valid. A recent news item published in the national press quotes two professors as saying that instructors who give better grades receive better student evaluations.[3, 4]

The papers referred to in the articles are part of a compendium of papers in which the question of student rating validity is discussed.[5] One of the papers (Greenwald & Gillmore) discusses leniency and notes that it is possible to normalize the ratings if this is thought to be a contaminant. All of the other authors publishing in this compendium disagree with the conclusion that leniency is a serious contaminant, and discussion papers appeared that also cast doubt on the validity of their conclusions.[6] The authors of one of the papers in the original compendium (Marsh & Roche) conducted a thorough review of student evaluation literature and presented their conclusions as shown in Table 7.1; my comments are in parentheses.

Their overall conclusion, matching the conclusions of many others, is that student ratings provide a valid and reproducible measure of teaching effectiveness, but that it is only one measure and other data such as observation are also useful.

Often the argument used to discredit student ratings (especially in research universities) is that student evaluations are meaningless because the only true measure of teaching skill is to ask for evaluations from students who have graduated some years back. The hypothesis is that only later in life will students realize from whom they learned the most and who the best teachers really were, and that asking students immediately after a course is finished favors those professors who by virtue of their pleasing personality or lack of course rigor will receive high ratings from students. But research has shown this hypothesis to be false. The data indicate that there is no significant change in teacher ratings with time. Students asked 10 and 20 years after graduation to name their best instructors will name the same instructors whom they rated highly while they were students. The tough instructors who had poor teaching skills regardless of how difficult their courses were are still rated poorly.[7]

Another indication that the opinion of teaching effectiveness does not change with time is the stories alumni tell of their best teachers. According to a recent research study, the instructors rated highly by students are also highly rated by alumni. This conclusion applied for both humanities and the sciences. When alumni were asked to describe their former professors, they told stories that illustrated the positive effect the teachers had on their lives. One alumnus, finishing his favorite story about his former professor, ended reflectively—"I miss him" he said—30 years after graduation.[8]

One attribute of excellent professors, especially in the natural and social sciences, is their ability to keep up with the developments in the field. An argument sometimes heard at research universities is that faculty should do research because that is what makes them better teachers. There

TABLE 7.1 Relationships Found Between Student Ratings and
Background Characteristics

Background Characteristic	Summary of Findings
Prior subject interest	A higher interest rate results in more favorable evaluations. (Comment: This is news? If students are interested in a course they work harder and get more out of it. Besides, how can we tell if the interest existed before the start of the course or was generated by the course or the instructor?)
Expected grade/actual grade	Class-average grades are correlated with class-average students. (Comment: How can we ever know if the higher grades were because of grading leniency, superior learning, or preexisting differences? If I get all of my students so excited about a course that they work very hard and learn a lot, why should I not give them all high grades?)
Reason for taking a course	Elective courses and those with a higher percentage of students taking the course for general interest tend to be rated higher.
Workload difficulty	Harder, more difficult courses requiring more effort and time are rated somewhat more favorably.
Class size	Most studies show smaller classes are rated somewhat more favorably. Some research shows that large classes are also rated more favorably. (Comment: Small classes tend to be upper-level seminars so that makes sense, and very large classes are often taught by master teachers who are teaching the course because they are such good teachers.)
Level of course or year	Graduate-level courses are rated somewhat more favorably, upper-division courses are rated somewhat higher than lower-division courses.
Instructor's rank	Little or no effect.
Sex of instructor or student	Little or no effect.
Academic discipline	Somewhat higher ratings in the humanities and lower ratings in the sciences.
Purpose of ratings	Somewhat higher if students know they are to be used for tenure or promotion.
Administrative conditions	Somewhat higher if ratings are not anonymous and if professor is present when ratings are being completed.
Student's personality	Little or no effect.

SOURCE: Marsh, H. W., & Roche, L. A. (1997). Making student evaluations of teaching effectiveness effective. *American Psychologist, 52*(11), 1187-1197.

is truth in this, since over the professional span of perhaps 40 years any discipline certainly will change, and a professor who does not change with it is hopelessly obsolete. Students, however, especially undergraduates, often cannot discriminate between an obsolete instructor and one who is at the cutting edge of the research, and they tend to give similar ratings to both instructors. In fact, the correlation between student ratings and level of research conducted by the professor is essentially zero, and there is little to the argument that doing research is necessary to be judged a good teacher by the students.[9] I believe it is necessary in many disciplines to do research to be a good instructor, but this does not appear to show up in student evaluations.

In spite of the evidence that student evaluations, at least in the aggregate, are statistically useful and not subject to irrelevant variables, some faculty disparage their use. Without trying to be unkind, it has been my experience that faculty who demean and bemoan student, course, and instructor evaluations as being unfair, biased, and unreliable are precisely the ones who get low ratings and decline to use the information on the evaluations to improve their teaching.

Considerable care should therefore be given to how these evaluations are conducted. Unfortunately, the common practice is to give students a form to fill out with very specific questions such as the following:

1. Were the objectives of the course made clear to you at the start of the course?
2. Were the tests graded fairly?
3. How much intellectual content did the course have?

Students are asked to respond usually on a scale of 1 to 5.

"But," protest the students, "these are not answerable on a scale of 1 to 5. We want to discuss these and tell you why we are answering the way we are." Research has shown that the best information on teaching can be obtained with small-group discussion with a facilitator (not the instructor).[10] The class can be divided into smaller discussion groups, and the facilitator would prepare the summary of the discussion. In this manner, the students are able to hear what others say and to remember important points that they might have forgotten when filling out the individual questionnaire. The summary discussions by the facilitators are then further summarized into a report of the course that not only is representative of all of the students but is a synthesis of the course. Most important, such a summary would be of greatest benefit to the instructor in modifying the course.

For beginning instructors, the best way to ensure that you will receive good student ratings at the end of a course is to ask for evaluations along the way. Have at least one mid-course evaluation, and take the students' concerns seriously. Do not wait until the end of the course to find that you were driving them crazy by some small distraction that you could easily have corrected. Make a habit of using some of the assessment techniques discussed in Chapter 3 to get continuous feedback on how the class is going.

Finally, if you then are lucky enough to get good ratings from your students, revel in those ratings. There is no better pat on the back than to be told by students that they have found your class to be valuable in their quest to be educated people.

Notes

1. Some professors argue that any dolt can get a good grade on an exam if given enough time and this is why they give timed tests where only the good students finish. I find this argument patently and obviously false. We should not be testing their speed but their knowledge.

2. Cashin, W. E. (1988). *Student ratings of teaching: A summary of the research.* IDEA Paper No. 20. Center for Faculty Evaluation and Development, Kansas State University.

3. Wilson, R. (1998, January 16). New research casts doubt on value of student evaluations of professors. *Chronicle of Higher Education,* p. A13.

4. Archibold, R. C. (1998, May 24). Give me an "A" or else. *New York Times.*

5. Marsh, H. W., & Roche, L. A. (1997). Making students' evaluations of teaching effectiveness effective. *American Psychologist, 52*(11), 1187-1197; d'Apollonia, S., & Abrami, P. Navigating student ratings of instructors. (1997). *American Psychologist, 52*(11), 1198-1208; Greenwald, A., & Gillmore, G. M. (1997). Grading lenience is a removable contaminant of student ratings. *American Psychologist, 52*(11), 1209-1217; McKeachie, W. J. (1997). Student ratings. *American Psychologist, 52*(11), 1218-1225.

6. Trout, P. A. (1997). What the numbers mean. *Change, 29*(5), 16-24.

7. Drucker, A. J., & Remmers, H. H. (1951). Do alumni and students differ in their attitudes toward instructors? *Journal of Educational Psychology, 42,* 129-143. Aleamoni, L. M., & Yimer, M. (1973). An investigation of the relationship between colleague rating, student rating, research productivity, and academic rank in rating instructional effectiveness. *Journal of Educational Psychology, 64,* 274-277.

8. Carson, B. H. Thirty years of stories. *Change, 28*(6), 10-17.

9. Centra, J. A. (1983). Research productivity and teaching effectiveness. *Research in Higher Education, 18,* 379-386.

10. Abbott, R., Wulff, D., Nyquist, J., Ropp, V. A., & Hess, C. (1990). Satisfaction with processes of collecting student opinions about instruction. *Journal of Educational Psychology, 83*(2), 201-206.

CHAPTER 8

Advising and Mentoring

Building the scaffolding to help students learn includes contact outside of class. Most often this is in the form of either informal or formal advising. In this chapter I discuss your responsibilities as an advisor to students.

Making Students Welcome

Your first job, as an advisor or as a mentor to graduate students, is to make sure that your students find it comfortable to come to you for advice. Often, students, especially freshmen, do not want to come to your office (that inner sanctum where unspeakable satanic rites are performed) but want to seek you out in less formal settings. One of these is before or after class. Good advisors will therefore make it a point to come early to a class and loiter around afterward.[1]

Another technique is to tell students that you can be found at some location on campus during some set time every week: "I will be at the Café on Wednesdays between 9 and 10 in the morning." Such a meeting is far less intimidating to the student because it is on neutral turf.

One way I found I could make students feel welcome in my office is similar to how my own children were taught to swim. They were thrown into the water. One year I assigned a paper to a large class and told my students that they were to write a paragraph proposal for the paper and then come to my office and discuss it with me. They all came, reluctantly. But they found that the meeting was not so bad and that I actually cared about their paper, and for the rest of the semester, I had no peace. Whenever they had a free moment, they would pop into my office to sit and talk. In retrospect, this may not have been such a bright idea.

Another way of making students feel welcome is to arrange your office in a non-intimidating way. The placement of office furniture is most important. If your desk faces the door as one enters, then there is an immediate confrontation between the visitor and desk occupant. In contrast, placing the desk along a side wall requires the professor to turn to meet the visitor—a much friendlier welcome.

Students seek out professors for a variety of reasons ranging from professional to personal. Sometimes the most and best an advisor can do is simply to be a sympathetic ear, to let the problem solve itself. At times, however, the student-professor relationship can take on complex overtones. May Sarton, in her book *The Small Room,* observes that "the relation between student and teacher must be about the most complex and ill-defined there is."[2] The student is searching for a way to relate on a person-person level to the instructor, and you are trying to maintain a friendly distance. You are neither *in loco parentis* nor an equal, and to make matters worse, you are vulnerable to whatever discussion topics are brought to you by the student.

The questions you can get from the student can range widely. Some questions are easy to handle, while others are very difficult. Although you are not advising the student in a professional capacity (as a psychologist would, for example), the student will want to believe that your conversation is in confidence. In the vast majority of cases, you should honor this assumption. In my opinion, confidentiality should be breached only if there is a real possibility of direct harm. For example, if a student starts talking about suicide, you are morally permitted and obligated to call the counseling service and ask for help.

Another problem can arise when the conversation with the student turns into a personal attack on another student or a professor. If you share the student's feelings toward the individual, it might be difficult to lead the conversation to a different topic. A most difficult situation occurs when a student starts to complain about another professor, and you know full well that everything he or she is saying is true. Nevertheless, your responsibility as a colleague is to not respond to the ad hominem attack, regardless of how justified. Depending on the situation, you might suggest that the student seek the help of the departmental chair or the dean, but you might feel like a hypocrite if you know full well that the chair or the dean will not do anything to rectify the situation.

Some leaders in the collegiate teaching profession strongly advise maintaining a strict businesslike relationship between the student and the instructor. Peter Markie advises that professors should not have any casual relationships with students, that such relationships "conflict with our fundamental obligations as professors."[3] Stephen Cahn argues that the ethics of the relationship require that the professor remain "dispassionate," avoiding any appearance of partiality. The professor, according to Cahn, should "not seek to be their psychiatrist, friend, or lover."[4]

I firmly agree with Cahn about the psychiatrist and lover part, but I am not sure about the evil of friendships between students and professors. Too often we tend to be overly cautious and to keep students at a distance, not offering them the encouragement and support they need. Joseph Katz observes that "there are far too many students in our courses for whom learning has been a humiliating experience. . . . It is remarkable in how many ways teachers unwittingly exacerbate [students'] lack of self-esteem."[5] One way of encouraging students to higher levels of achievement is to offer friendship as a part of your professorial role.

Richard Baker, in a wonderful description of May Sarton's *The Small Room,* presents a convincing case for friendship between professor and student. There are times and situations, he argues, when friendship is exactly what is needed in the mentoring relationship. Such a friendship does not have to be destructive or result in unjust impartiality. A small note of encouragement, a friendly gesture, making time during a busy schedule for "hanging out," asking an underachieving student to chat, answering email, paying attention to their extracurricular activities and achievements, . . . these are all indicators of friendship, and they mean a great deal to students. As Baker concludes, "The key ethical point . . . is that the professor—both inside and outside the classroom—should act as a friend."[6]

But there is a difference between "friend" and "pal." Remember that you as the teacher/professor have a special power relationship with the student. You will be called on to evaluate performance and to do so "dispassionately," using Cahn's word. You cannot be a pal, shooting hoops with your students and drinking beer afterwards, or joining them in dancing the night away at a sorority ball. By trying to be a pal, you will destroy the fragile relationship that is such an integral part of education.

Student-Specific Advising

Your relationships with students must be student-specific because different students need different kinds of advising and mentoring. Sometimes you can pick up clues on what they need most in advising, but sometimes you can use gross generalizations to give you an initial advantage. For example, there is a significant gender difference in what students expect from an advisor, as shown in the Table 8.1.

Although this is statistically a stunning difference, be careful about generalization. More men than women want concrete and directive suggestions, but a significant fraction of women do expect such help. Similarly, one third of the men expect the professor to take the time to get to know them personally. What this means to you as an advisor is that if you are to serve the students' needs, all students should be treated as individuals. Get to know your students and allow them to lead the way in conference.

Another difference you have to be aware of is in the advising needs of some minority students. A study conducted by the Society for Values in Higher Education found that "mentoring minority students required more time than mentoring other students. Additional time [is] required to develop an atmosphere of continually growing trust in order to bring out crucial information about personal and intellectual backgrounds, values, and aspirations."[7]

Some students have special needs that demand consideration and attention. Physical disabilities can prevent doing manual work such as laboratories, for example, and special arrangements must be made. More difficult to handle are learning disabilities, which differ from physical disabilities in that they are not obvious. They can challenge the instructor in developing modified student assessment procedures. The National Joint Committee on Learning Disabilities defines learning disabilities in this way:

TABLE 8.1 What Students Expect From an Advisor

Fraction of Male and Female Students Who Expect an Advisor to . . .	Male	Female
. . . take time to know me personally.	30	72
. . . share my interests so that we have something in common.	31	58
. . . know where to send me to get information.	48	51
. . . know the facts about the courses.	64	43
. . . make concrete and directive suggestions.	66	23

SOURCE: Light, R. J. (1990). *The Harvard assessment seminars.* Cambridge, MA: Harvard University Press.

Learning disabilities is a general term that refers to a heterogeneous group of disorders manifested by significant difficulties in the acquisition and use of listening, speaking, reading, writing, reasoning, or mathematical abilities. These disorders are intrinsic to the individual, presumed to be due to central nervous dysfunction, and may occur across the life span. Problems in self-regulatory behaviors, social precedent, and social interaction may exist with learning disabilities but do not by themselves constitute a learning disability. Although learning disabilities may occur concomitantly with other handicapping conditions (for example, sensory impairment, mental retardation, serious emotional disturbance) or with extrinsic influences (such as cultural differences, insufficient or inappropriate instruction), they are not the result of those conditions or influences.[8]

Another condition that can affect a student's learning is Attention Deficit Disorder (ADD), which is similar to a learning disability and requires individual attention, especially in testing. Basically, students with ADD cannot concentrate on a single task for very long. This condition may include hyperactivity and restlessness.

You will learn of students with learning disabilities in one of two ways. You may begin to suspect that a student in your class who appears to be bright and otherwise perfectly normal is having great difficulty taking tests. He or she may do wonderful work on homework assignments and projects but simply cannot get good scores on tests. If this occurs, you should discuss the situation with the student and suggest that he or she visit the counseling service. The counseling service may find that the student has a form of learning disability that makes it difficult to take examinations, for example, and the counseling service can provide help that will reduce the effect of this disability.

The other way you can find out about learning disabilities is through a letter from the counseling service that alerts you that a student has such problems. Of course, this should be kept strictly confidential, but you must make accommodations for this student. Often, simply allowing the student more time on exams or allowing him or her to take exams alone in a conference room is the best alternative. Talk to the student and develop a mutual agreement as to how this problem can best be resolved.

I say in the above paragraph that you *must* do this because it is, in fact, federal law that you do. Section 504 of the Rehabilitation Act of 1973 specifically states that "no otherwise qualified handicapped individual in the United States shall, solely by reason of his handicap, be excluded from the participation in, be denied the benefits of, or be subjected to discrimination under any program or activity receiving federal financial assistance." But even if it were not law, any sense of fairness or compassion would lead you to provide the best accommodation to those who have special disabilities.

There is a personal caveat to this, however. The counseling services, when they do their testing for learning disabilities, will not report the *extent* of these disabilities, but will only report a "yes" or "no." That is, if the disability is severe enough, the student is judged to have the problem; if it is not quite that severe, the student is judged to not have the problem. This bifurcation might be logical for the clinical psychologist, but for the faculty, it presents special problems. Learning disabilities are not, of course, like pregnancies. Students with learning disabilities can be slightly disabled.

Such "yes" or "no" reporting, however, leads to two problems for you as the instructor. First, you may suspect that a student has a disability, but the counseling center may refuse to confirm it, meaning that the problem is simply not severe enough to cross the line. Such cases require Solomon-like decisions, and you can be placed in uncomfortable positions. Even more difficult is the situation when a student is classified as having a learning disability and then takes great glee in using the classification to get out of work or to receive special considerations. In my experience, this is a rare instance, but I did have a student who stopped coming to class the day he was classified as having a learning disability, claiming that he was just too learning disabled to make it to lecture. A phone call to the counseling service confirmed my suspicion that the disability had nothing whatever to do with classroom attendance, and I had to use my most forceful manner to straighten the student out before the convenient disability classification could do him some real damage. I would very much like to have the counseling services provide more than just a "yes" or "no" designation for students, and maybe eventually we can get around to that. In the meantime, as an instructor, you have to be aware of and compassionate toward the students who truly have learning disabilities and make every accommodation to help them attain their fair share of a university education.

Responding to Personal Problems

One of the most difficult advising situations occurs when students come to you with serious personal problems. The best option is for you to recommend that the student seek professional counseling from the university counseling service. This advice is to the benefit of both the student and the professor, and you have an ethical responsibility not to try to do amateur psychiatry. You may want to have the telephone of the university counseling service handy to give to the student in need, and at times you may want to call the counselor yourself and explain the situation. Never ignore symptoms of depression or threats of suicide.

Sometime during your career, you may have a student who develops a crush on you. First and foremost, do not encourage such behavior (see Chapter 13 on how to get fired). But remember that students are people with deep feelings and that they need to be taken seriously. If a situation like this develops, arrange a private talk with the student in a public place and explain why the student's feelings are not and will not be reciprocated. Be kind and understanding, but firm. You may also want to make sure that you never find yourself alone with this student in a private place such as your office. If an uncomfortable situation develops in your office, simply get up and open the office door. The message should be clear. Some instructors *always* keep their office doors open just to prevent the possibility of a student claiming that something untoward had happened in the office.

Mentoring

As a young faculty member with graduate students, you will have some interesting interactions. You will not be too much older than the students and they will have a hard time calling you "Doctor," but they also (at least in most universities) will not feel comfortable calling you by your first name.[9]

But at the same time, you will be a mentor for them, especially for students who begin to work in your laboratory and are funded by your grants, and for the teaching assistants assigned to you. Being a mentor is more difficult than being an advisor. As an advisor, you relinquish your role when the student graduates. A mentor never quits—kind of like being a parent.

Mentoring Ph.D. students is the most work and the most fun. You watch him or her grow up in front of your eyes and revel in the day when for the first time the student challenges you on your own turf. Often he or she is right and you are wrong, and you realize that the student is evolving into a colleague.

Mentoring Ph.D. students has many facets. Not only are you to teach them how to do good scholarship, but you have to show them how to write papers, make presentations, and generally survive in the academic world. One of the most difficult and time-consuming challenges (especially for overseas students) is teaching them to write. Often this responsibility is overlooked, or you might find that just writing the stuff for the student is easier and faster than correcting his or her poorly written work. Such neglect is an abrogation of your duty as a mentor, however, and you should accept the responsibility of teaching writing along with teaching research and scholarship.

As all of us know, at some time during the third year of the Ph.D. program, the student is faced with what appears to be the impossibility of the task. Nothing seems to work. There is no sense to the experiments, and the data are not falling into place. The argument that you thought was brilliant during the proposal defense is now full of holes. You begin to wonder if this is really what you want to do with your life. Do I really want to go bashing my head against the wall? There are no deadlines— just impossibly difficult and time-consuming research with no end in sight.

Some mentors call this time the "black hole," the depressing time experienced in the course of every Ph.D. who ever undertook the task.[10] Your responsibility as the mentor is to get students through this terrible time. Take them to lunch, take a long walk, let them unload on you, listen, be sympathetic, and perhaps most important, tell them about your own "black hole." Give them assurance that it can be done.

What are the attributes of a good mentor? What do students look for? Some anthropology graduate students at the University of Illinois developed a mentor appreciation program in which students nominate their mentors for public recognition.[11] Their criteria for being a good mentor are excellent. They suggest that the quality of a mentor be judged on the basis of:

- **Technical academic advising**
  Transmitting knowledge, methods, and scientific rigor
  Giving educational direction and referral
  Providing thoughtful critiques of submitted work
- **Ethical professional standards**
  Stimulating critical thinking by setting a standard of rigorous and thorough knowledge of the field
  Transmitting professional ethical behavior
  Sharing professional development
- **Professional relationship**
  Being attentive to the needs of the student and able to respond to diverse needs
  Stimulating independent work through encouragement and development of student's ideas and interests
  Balancing the reciprocal relationship, often reflected in accessibility
  Displaying consistent, professional guidance regarding larger career decisions and opportunities (e.g., conferences, papers, fieldwork, grants, new publication, jobs, and professional contacts)

That is quite a list. Quite a responsibility.

Notes

1. Contrast this with many European lectures where the class is assembled and the instructor walks in, the students rise, and the lecture begins. When the lecture is over, the students rise, and the professor leaves. There is no personal contact.
2. Sarton, M. (1961). *The small room.* New York: Norton.
3. Markie, P. (1994). *A professor's duties* (p. 74). Lanham, MD: Rowman & Littlefield.

4. Cahn, S. (1986). *Saints and sinners: Ethics in academia* (p. 35). Totowa, NH: Rowman & Littlefield.

5. Katz, J. (1988). Does teaching help students learn? In B. A. Kimball (Ed.), *Teaching undergraduates* (p. 177). Buffalo, NY: Prometheus.

6. Baker, R., Jr. (1996, Summer). Ethics of student-faculty friendship. In L. Fisch (Ed.), *Ethical dimensions of college and university teaching: Understanding and honoring the special relationship between teachers and students* (New directions for teaching and learning, No. 66, p. 32). San Francisco: Jossey-Bass.

7. Smith, D. (1996, Summer). The ethics of teaching. In L. Fisch (Ed.), *Ethical dimensions of college and university teaching: Understanding and honoring the special relationship between teachers and students* (New directions for teaching and learning, No. 66, p. 10). San Francisco: Jossey-Bass.

8. Hammill, D. D. (1988). A new definition of learning disabilities. *Learning Disabilities Quarterly, 11*(3), 217-223.

9. It took me 10 years after graduation before I could muster up the courage to call my mentor, Dr. Daniel Okun, by his first name.

10. Kramer, R. M., & Martin, J. (1996). Transition and turning points in faculty-doctoral student relationships. In P. J. Frost & M. S. Taylor (Eds.), *Rhythms of academic life*. Thousand Oaks, CA: Sage.

11. With thanks to Lauren Sieg, University of Illinois.

CHAPTER 9

Research and Scholarship

When a university interviews you for a job, the conversation often turns to how quickly you can win the Nobel or Pulitzer Prize. After all, the Ph.D. degree is not a license to teach—it is a certificate attesting to your ability to perform independent scholarship at a high level.

In this chapter, I discuss the justification for the research bias of many universities. Then I discuss the decision we all have to make on what research or scholarly activity we want to undertake. Finally, I look at the question of funding for research, particularly in the sciences and in engineering.

Why Universities Emphasize Research and Published Scholarship

As noted in Chapter 1, published research drives university administrators because this is how the universities and their administrators earn their reputations. This is also why so much undergraduate tuition is used to underwrite research and other scholarly activities. A notch or two in national rankings is a life or death issue, and schools do not climb the ladder by promoting excellence in teaching, advising, or other undergraduate pursuits, a fact that is increasingly apparent even at nonresearch colleges and universities.[1]

At research universities, the most important criterion for tenure is publications. In the sciences and engineering, publications are usually difficult to produce unless expensive research work is conducted, and this requires outside or external funding. At the comprehensive and baccalaureate colleges and universities, external funding is increasingly necessary for promotion and tenure. If you are in the sciences or engineering, your career may be dependent on your ability to find external financing.

In the humanities, where publication can still be a single-minded scholarly activity, one can still cloister oneself in the library and emerge years later, like a butterfly from a cocoon, with a brilliant book that will earn tenure. Far better, however, is to seek funding for independent study during graduate school or to work as a post-doc without the burden of teaching classes while turning the dissertation into a book. No matter what your field and no matter where you will be working, you will be expected (encouraged) to find external funding.

Universities emphasize external funding for two reasons. First, such funds allow research and other scholarly activity to be conducted, and this increases the visibility and reputation of the institute. The second reason is that such external funding has built into it overhead, or "free money." This is not free money, of course, and every external research dollar obtained is heavily subsidized by undergraduate tuition.

Most administrators will contend that tuition does not subsidize research, but there are two strong arguments to prove that this is the case. The first argument is based on the tuition paid by undergraduate students at various institutions. In 1996, the tuition for private research universities and colleges averaged more than $17,000 annually, while the baccalaureate colleges charged only about $12,000. What is this $5,000 used for? It certainly is not used for better undergraduate classrooms. The quality of laboratories in comprehensive universities and colleges seems to be as good as or better than the ones in the research universities. Is it to pay for more student services? These seem to be about equal. Where then does this money go? It has to go to subsidize the research at the universities, the only real difference between the two institutions.

The second argument comes from the overhead that universities are able to charge to the federal government. Typically, a research university might charge 50% overhead. That is, if a faculty member writes a grant proposal for research that will cost $100,000 to do, the final cost to the funding agency is $150,000. The university keeps the $50,000 to pay for the upkeep of the buildings, power and heat, and so on. But if a non-university, not-for-profit organization writes a proposal to the federal government, it is allowed to charge as much as 120% overhead. That is, on a \$100,000 project, it costs the organization \$120,000 just to pay for all the ancillary support services. If it truly takes \$120,000 to pay for the support, and if the university can charge only \$50,000, where does the \$70,000 difference come from? Only one source: undergraduate tuition (or alumni contributions—money that would otherwise have gone to benefit education and thus lowered the tuition).

Undergraduates do not get upset about this because the research conducted by the faculty enhances the reputation of the university, and their degrees will be worth more to them in the long run than similar degrees from non-research-centered universities. Nobody is complaining. It just bothers me that we are not truthful with our students. We should say, "This fraction of your tuition goes to pay for instruction, and this much goes to subsidize faculty research."

Experience has shown that the path of subsidizing faculty research is the path to success. By using this scheme, such formerly sleepy colleges as Duke University have been able to achieve great fame and success, and students are very pleased with their experiences at Duke. Would they be upset to know that about 15% of their \$100,000 tuition is used to support research by faculty they have never seen and who never contributed toward their education? Probably not.

Securing external funding to expand research is a successful formula, and more and more colleges are trying to get aboard the bandwagon. As you prepare to start your career, count on having to find external funding so that you can please the administrators who make tenure and promotion decisions. But to obtain external funding, you have to have something to sell. You have to choose a research or scholarly topic.

Choosing the Topic for Research or Scholarship

Most young professors do not make fresh decisions about their first research topic or scholarly area of interest but simply expand on their Ph.D. topic since this is the easiest area to attack within the few years before tenure review. At some point, however, you have the opportunity to decide what you study next, that is, what scholarly work you shall ask the university to help fund.

Peter Markie suggests that choosing a research topic should not be a value-free decision.[2] We have a moral obligation, according to Markie, to "engage in scholarship that supports our teaching by maintaining and increasing our knowledge in what we teach." That is, a professor who teaches only undergraduate philosophy courses should not research the life and times of some obscure philosopher. Such scholarship would not be directly applicable to the teaching and should not be done on company time. Similarly, if a civil engineering professor has no responsibilities in teaching classes or even sections of classes in art history, he or she should not participate in such scholarly endeavors, except as a hobby.

This view is harsh, and perhaps a bit too restrictive. Studying the obscure philosopher can provide new insights into philosophy generally and improve teaching by providing greater breadth in the field. A civil engineer who understands and appreciates art history would be a far more valuable teacher of structural engineering, perhaps sprinkling lectures with interesting stories and examples of ancient building technology. I believe that a professor in one discipline crossing over into another to do scholarly research is not nearly as antithetical to the ideas and ideals of a university than a professor who has stopped learning altogether. We are, after all, role models for our students and we should demonstrate to them the excitement of lifelong learning.

Choosing the Funding Agency

Three kinds of funds are available to universities. *Contracts* are written between the funding agency and the university to accomplish a specific goal that a funding agency has in mind. Suppose the Environmental Protection Agency wants to build a better outhouse. It selects a university and then signs an agreement with it to do the analysis and design and to report back within a specified time. The EPA program officer would have tight control over the project and the university has little leeway in how it spends the money. In this way, the university is in competition with hundreds of research institutes and companies that feed out of the governmental trough. There is, in fact, some question as to the ethical validity of this type of funding, because the university, a not-for-profit enterprise that does not pay taxes, is in direct competition with private companies and research organizations, a situation not dissimilar to a religious organization owning and operating a business.

The second form of funding is *grants*. Grants are given to universities for much less specific work, and there is considerable leeway in how the money can be spent as long as it is in the general area of the specified research. The only requirement in the end is to show that the research group has published the results in journals, demonstrating that the research has been competently done. Both contracts and grants carry full overhead, the multiplier used to pay the university for the use of its facilities and services.

The third form of external funding is *gifts*. Gifts are the best kind of funding to the faculty because gifts have no strings attached whatsoever. Gifts also do not pay overhead, so that the entire sum comes to the researcher and no money goes to the university. Obviously, universities are not keen on having too many gifts flowing into the university, since they would have to make up an even greater percentage of the cost of doing research from undergraduate tuition dollars.

Sources of external funds are either governmental or nongovernmental. For sciences and engineering, the National Science Foundation is the great sugar daddy. The NSF also does ethics (of sciences), and hence even philosophers can obtain funding from this source. For health-related and biotechnology work, the National Institutes of Health is the largest single contributor. For the humanities, the National Endowment for the Humanities will give smaller grants, but this agency has had some rough years with the Republican Congress, and its future is in doubt. Other agencies that fund research include the Department of Defense, the Department of Energy, and the Atomic Energy Commission.

In the private sector, funding is almost exclusively from foundations, ranging from the biggies like the Rockefeller Foundation and Ford Foundation to much smaller ones that target specific areas of interest.

Both types of funding sources will periodically publish a "request for proposals" (RFP) that spells out what areas of research they are interested in supporting. If you believe that there is a good match between your area of expertise and the RFP, you would then respond by writing a proposal. But your chances of getting funded are pretty slim using this technique, because every university and research institute is keeping up with the governmental RFPs, and they have armies of proposal writers ready to pounce on the next one that even comes close to what they do.

A better technique is to respond to a "program announcement" as published by the NSF and other agencies. These announcements spell out in vague terms what they are interested in. You have a far better chance of being successful, because the competition will be with other universities and not with private research organizations.

The best technique (as your advisor will tell you) is to get to know the program officers, the people who are most responsible for how the agency funds are spent. I have been on panels where it became very obvious what the program officer wanted to do, and the panel complied. The program officer can also orchestrate the external reviews, so that if good ones are needed, good ones will be received, and if bad reviews are sought, such will be received. The program officers do not do this out of maliciousness, of course. They have the best handle on what would be considered good research and will try to influence the decision accordingly. Getting to know the program officer in an agency, listening to this person, and following his or her suggestions leads to a high percentage of successful proposals funded.

Writing Your Proposal

There are books and books written on how to write good research proposals, and I cannot begin to list all the tips for writing good proposals here. I can, however, summarize the attributes of good proposals. To succeed, you must make sure that the project is interesting and worthwhile and that the proposal is readable and understandable

I can say little about the first attribute because this is discipline-specific. In all proposals, however, the trick is to catch the attention of the reviewer. Always start by telling the reader why this proposal is the best thing since sliced bread. How will the study change the field or change the direction of scholarship? What wonderful new knowledge will we discover if this research is done, and why this is needed if the field is to move forward? Assume that the evaluator is fully knowledgeable about the field and will agree with you that this study is an exciting new direction for the discipline.

The second attribute of a good proposal is too often ignored and deserves emphasis. If the evaluators cannot understand what you intend to do, or if the prose is painful to read, the proposal will be rejected. Remember that the reviewers are busy people who do not have a lot of time to waste on reading carelessly prepared proposals. Negative vibes build as soon as the reader encounters bad grammar, misspelled words, loose organization, missing parts of the proposal, or turgid writing. The best of ideas can end up on the reject pile if poorly expressed.

To avoid this fate, get help. The best help comes from your mentors and colleagues. They have all either served on proposal review committees or reviewed journal papers. They can be of immense help in pointing out weaknesses in your proposal or identifying poorly written passages. Arrange with your colleagues to read each other's proposals and then have an honest and critical discussion of them. Talk about presentation as well as substance.

The secondary benefit from such collegial cooperation is that all of you will learn to write better proposals. If you continue to get hammered by your colleagues on writing style, for example, you will soon see the error of your ways and improve. Or if you are not careful in outlining the statistical methods to be used in the reduction of your data, you will become more careful in how you discuss this in future proposals. It is always better to get the blood on the floor within your academic group instead of having your proposal bleed in the evaluation process.

Getting Your Proposal Funded

So here is the system: You work and you write and you agonize for weeks preparing a proposal to do some first-rate scholarly stuff. When the proposal is received, the program officer sends copies of it to a list of people he or she believes would be able to offer reviews of the proposal. You do not know who these people are, and you cannot control this selection. Once the external reviews are in, your proposal is judged by a panel, set up by the program officer for reviewing a whole pile of proposals and providing the program officer guidance on which to fund. Using the external reviews and presenting oral arguments for or against funding, the panel develops a priority ranking. People who sit on this panel are usually from your discipline, but again you have no knowledge or choice of who will do the judging. Worse, you have no chance to defend yourself. The decisions are sub rosa, and if your proposal is misunderstood or misinterpreted, too bad.

The panel creates a list of proposals it would like to see funded. The program officer then uses this list as a guide and allocates whatever money is available to the funding of as many of the proposals as possible, sometimes at a reduced level. Because your success depends so much on the luck of the draw and who reads your submission, you write lots of proposals, hoping that at least some of them will be funded. This, of course, takes time and money, and fully 10% of your time will be spent in proposal writing, while a large fraction of your university resources are spent on identifying potential funding sources and preparing zillions of copies of proposals.

There has to be a better way. Unfortunately, there isn't. Look at the alternatives. Suppose a committee of uninformed politicians doles out the money? Or some single person (Plato's philosopher king?) who is so smart and insightful that he or she chooses only the best proposals? Or why not a lottery?—choose a number and pick a numbered ball out of a tub.

There just does not appear to be a better way. It still makes sense to have experts judge proposals on their scholarly merit, even if these experts might have prejudices, biases, histories of personal conflict, or debts to pay. We are, at least for the present, stuck with the system that can be unfair, expensive, and cumbersome, but which on the whole produces the best results.

I do not want to indict the proposal reviewers. Whether external reviewers or panel members who get together to provide guidance to the program officer on which proposal to review, all the people I have met and worked with have been upstanding, dedicated, and fair human beings. You will also someday be asked to judge proposals or to sit on panels and you will see how subjective the system is. But for the most part, the really well-thought-through proposals that promise to produce significant new findings will get funded and the shoddy fly-by-night proposals will not. But mistakes will also be made.

Suppose your brilliant effort is one of those mistakes. Your proposal was not funded. You have two choices: Throw it in the trash or recycle it. **RECYCLE IT!** Faculty at universities that live on outside funding will resubmit their proposals an average of 15 times before they finally give up on them. Use the comments you received from the external reviewers and studiously modify your proposal to take these criticisms into account. Often the program officer will send your resubmitted proposal to the same reviewers and they will be pleased that you have followed their suggestions (regardless of how inane they might have been). Remember that getting external funds is largely a crap shoot, and it depends heavily on who reads your proposal and who makes the final decision. It might take you a few iterations to convince the reviewers and the decision maker that you do indeed have a wonderful idea and that you really are capable of doing first-rate research.

Notes

1. The dreaded *U.S. News and World Report* rankings, for example, include as one of their primary metrics the student-to-faculty ratio, a figure that can be inflated by hiring research professors who do not teach but who pay their own way through research contracts. Hiring self-supported researchers therefore can enhance rankings without spending university resources (or enhancing undergraduate education).

2. Markie, P. J. (1994). *Professor's duties: Ethical issues in college teaching.* Lanham, MD: Rowman & Littlefield.

CHAPTER 10

Publishing

About half of all the faculty in 4-year colleges have *never* published a scholarly paper in a professional journal.[1] But that is an irrelevant statistic. Research, scholarship, and publishing are required of all young professors at 4-year universities. This is also becoming true for teaching colleges, community colleges, or 2-year colleges. Even though these non-research institutions might not demand publication, you will quickly discover that those who publish receive the promotions and pay increases. Regardless of the academic job, it is greatly advantageous to publish.

You should start publishing early. When you graduate with a Ph.D., you should have several publications already in press or in the can. Such publications can be a strong argument during your job search. Experience has shown that if new assistant professors do not publish during the first few years on the job, they most likely never will. The least marketable Ph.D. is one with several years of experience and no publications. As Arthur Bedeian notes, "a new Ph.D.'s market value is generally greater than that of a seasoned Ph.D. who has yet to publish. The former, at least, offers potential. The latter can only offer excuses."[2]

You have to publish, whether or not you have anything important to say. But let's not be so negative or cynical. Publishing can be fun. The first time you see your name in print is a rush. There it is. You have written something others find worthwhile. And it will be there forever. You and your kids can always go to the library and find the publication. You have arrived.

In this chapter, I first discuss the mechanics of writing a paper and give some practical suggestions for writing technical and scholarly papers. Then I follow the process of a paper as it gets from your word processor to the final printed form in the journal. The sticky question of authorship is covered next, followed by some words on writing books.

How to Write a Scholarly Paper

The first step in writing is to define the subject and purpose of the communication. One suggestion is to start with the words "I want to tell you that . . ." and then cross them out when the paper is finished. After defining the subject and purpose you might even realize that the topic isn't worth pursuing (the ultimate brevity!).

Next, define the audience. Who will read the paper, and what would they want to learn from your paper? These questions will suggest the most appropriate journal for the paper. If you are unsure, read the *Guide to Authors* published by every respectable journal, usually in the last issue of the year, but sometimes in every issue. Typically such instructions will cover the following:

Subject areas. This is a statement describing the kinds of papers the journal seeks. The statement should say if the journal wants original only research or if it will accept case histories or review papers. Some journals will even print previously published papers that may have appeared in proceedings or other publications not normally available to the general public.

Language. English has become the lingua franca, although some international journals accept papers in major languages such as French or German.

Copyrights. Most journals now insist that the papers they publish be copyrighted. This has become important because of the use of coursepaks by faculty who collect papers and use these instead of or as a supplement to a textbook. Copy services now have to obtain permissions for all papers, and if the journal owns the copyright, it makes money every time the paper is used in a coursepak.

You can, of course, refuse to sign over the copyright to the journal, and I know of some professors who get away with it. If the paper is a good one, most journals will publish it regardless. Some will not. As a young faculty member, you have no real incentive or professional clout to refuse to sign over the copyright. What in effect the agreement says is that this paper may not be reproduced anywhere else without the publisher's permission. If you as the author want to use some of the figures or even major content of the paper in another publication, such as a book, there is nothing to keep you from doing so. In effect, the signing over of the copyright has no bearing on your use of your own material in the future.

Submission of manuscripts. Here you learn how many copies to submit, where to send them, and what to do with figures or other graphics. Often the journals will insist on a certain font or size and double spacing. Most journals also insist on receiving a computer disk with the text. Typically, science and engineering journals will require an abstract and key words.

Most important (for you, in terms of time) is the form of the references or citations. You should be aware of the different methods of citing (see below) and follow the guidelines. An even better idea is to look at the requirements before you actually prepare the paper. Tedious stuff—retyping references.

So now you know where you intend to send your paper and are ready to write it. There is no "best way" to write. Writing is highly individual-istic. While some authors labor for days over a single paragraph, others write entire books in a week. There is no one rigid writing process. Nevertheless, here are some pointers that may be useful for beginning writers of scholarly articles.

Prepare an outline. Try to get the central ideas into the outline and develop a logic of thought. Do the ideas flow and form a complete argument? Some writers purposely use a tiny sheet of paper for the initial outline to prevent them from spending a lot of time refining it.

Sketch all the graphs and other illustrations. It is always easier to write with the drawings spread out, just as it is easier to give a talk using slides.

Write. Move it! Do not wait for the proper construction, do not search for just the right word. Get everything down on paper. If the piece is lengthy, do not start at the beginning. Start writing the easiest part first, then move to the more difficult sections. In project reports, for example, the procedures and methods should be the simplest to write, so start with those.

The first sentence of your paper is the most important sentence. Do not start your paper with a well-worn cliché such as "The activated sludge system is a widely used method of . . ." or "There has been considerable development in learning theory during the past 10 years . . ." or "Research has shown that the Freundlich isotherm fits many types of adsorption data. . . ." For the fun of it, take any technical or science journal, copy all the first sentences in the papers, and then try to match the titles with the first sentences. I guarantee it will not be easy. Start your paper with something useful and interesting. Tell the reader why he or she should read your paper.

Edit. Edit in a rough way. Look for missing ideas, poor transitions, or convoluted construction.

Cool it. Try to put it aside for as long as possible; two weeks is the minimum for most writers, but in a pinch even a few hours can help.

Share it. If possible, have others read the piece and make suggestions for improvement. Sometimes the most obvious mistakes slip by until someone points them out.

Edit as a critical reader. With sufficient cooling, the material should read like someone else's writing. This is the chance to be especially critical of your own writing. The more time you can spend on a piece of writing, especially with large cooling periods interspersed, the better the product will be.

Each journal has its own style for references, so be sure to type the references in the required style. Some journals insist that you number all references consecutively as they appear in the text. Thus the first reference encountered is Number 1, usually as a superscript. The references in the list of references are then numbered consecutively. Other journals require that all references be listed in alphabetical order based on the author's last name and the reference numbers in the text correspond to the reference list.

A third method for references is to use the author's last name and publication date in parentheses. The primary advantage of this technique is that revisions do not require reference renumbering. The reference list is arranged alphabetically by author's last name, unnumbered, and revision involves simple additions or deletions.

Finally, some journals (and even scholarly fields) use footnotes and bibliographies. Typically the footnotes are consecutively numbered, and the footnoted material is found at the bottom of the page. Again, follow the guidelines of the journal as you begin to write your paper to avoid having to revise the citations.

One more note about references: When you use material from a paper in a lecture, or in an article you are writing, *copy the reference in its entirety.* The hours you will waste later when you use the reference and have to chase down the date or the author's initials or whatever will be some of the most useless hours of your professional life. Take it from one who has done it. Copy the whole citation in detail, including the page numbers. You will be eternally grateful to yourself.

Some writers will use software packages such as *Endnote* to store all of the references and have them available when they write a paper. In precomputer days we would do the same with index cards, keeping drawers full of the cards and being able to sort and alphabetize as needed. If you are a personality type who can take the time to keep a bibliographic software package up-to-date, then this is highly recommended. For the rest of us, remember to copy the reference in its entirety.

Submitting Your Paper for Publication

Suppose you have written your paper, carefully using the required citation style and reproducing the required number of copies. You include a cover letter to the editor stating the obvious—that you are submitting this paper for consideration. Let's follow the course of your paper after it arrives at the journal editor's desk.

But first, whatever you do, do not send the same paper for review by different journals at the same time. Most guides for authors state explicitly that only papers that have not been simultaneously submitted elsewhere will be reviewed. If you are caught submitting the same paper to two different journals (and this can happen if a reviewer is sent the same paper for review by two different journals), you will never again publish a paper in those journals. (Submitting book manuscripts is different, as noted later in this chapter.)

Typically, the first review is by the journal editor, who looks at the title and perhaps reads the abstract to determine if the subject matter is appropriate for the journal. The editor makes no value judgement at this point or shouldn't make a value judgment. (Editors are often very powerful and can reject your paper with no external review, and you have no appeal.)[3]

If the subject matter is appropriate, the editor will send your paper out for review. Each journal has a stable of reviewers who routinely read the submitted manuscripts. Typically they are chosen by the editor and are qualified to evaluate your paper because they also publish or do research in your area—hence the term *peer review*. This system, of course, is open to great abuse by unscrupulous reviewers. They can, if they so wish, delay your paper until they themselves have had the opportunity to do the research and to submit their own paper. Or the reviewer can give the paper such a bad review that the journal editor would not dare publish it.

Of course, the editor knows the game rules, as well as the names and numbers of all the players. If the journal editor wants to, he or she can kill any paper by simply sending it to reviewers likely to be unsympathetic to your approach. Conversely, the editor can send your paper to people who have never in their lives submitted a bad review and will most certainly like your paper as well.

The reviewers read the paper (often asking some of their graduate students to comment on it as well) and write the review. During this review, in the sciences, the reviewers evaluate the currency, accuracy, and validity of the results, looking for missed references and questionable interpretations. In the humanities, the reviewers judge the importance of the paper to the scholarly discussion in the area and evaluate the quality of the scholarship.

The editor collects these reviews and along with a personal assessment, sends the result to you. Typically, the verdict is one of four options:

1. Publish as is
2. Publish with minor revisions

3. Publish with major revisions
   a. does not have to be sent back for review
   b. must be sent back for another review
4. Do not publish

Some journals also publish technical notes, and sometimes the decision is to recommend that the paper be boiled down to a short note which would then be published. You do not want to do this, since the technical note is not considered a "full-length peer reviewed journal article"—the only animal that counts in your tenure review. Technical notes should be an option only if your paper has been rejected by all of the appropriate journals.

If the decision is to publish with or without minor revisions, then you have done a good job in preparing the paper. More than likely, however, you will receive a "publish with major revisions." Now you read the reviews, and you immediately recognize that

1. the reviewers are idiots, and/or
2. the reviewers have misunderstood the paper.

Perhaps, but probably not. Probably you missed something, or did not explain something very well, or did not see another side to the data, or missed something that actually would make your paper much better. The first impulse, however, is often to assume that you have been unfairly and unkindly treated by the reviewers and to strike back. Ah, the letter you can compose in your head to tell them where to get off! Resist that impulse. Try to see what they saw or did not see in your paper. Then write a cordial (even supplicating) response, telling the editor all the changes you made in response to the excellent and helpful comments by the reviewers. Do not, under any circumstances, pick a fight with the editor by claiming that the reviewers were idiots. Being nice works.

Remember to *expect* negative reviews. Most reviewers believe their job is to cut the paper apart and to provide reasons for why it should not be published. Only then do they think they are doing their job. Negative (and sometimes outright cruel) reviews are the norm. As Alan Meyer suggests, "If you want positive feedback, I recommend a dog."[4]

If you have responded adequately to those idiots . . . sorry, . . . to your reviewers, the editor will approve your paper for publication. At that point, your paper leaves the editor's desk and goes into production, which begins with copyediting (correcting spelling, punctuation, grammar, style, syntax, etc.). Typically, the journal copy editors read your paper and send you a copyedited version of it, at which point you immediately recognize that

1. the copy editors are idiots, and/or
2. the copyeditors are incompetent.

Perhaps, but more than likely they really do know the difference between "which" and "that," and you might even learn something yourself. Most important, they do not decide journal policy. If, for example, the journal does not permit the use of first-person singular "I," then no amount of arguing with the copy editor will work. Or if the journal insists on placing the period at the end of the sentence inside the quotation marks (an anachronistic practice), accept this with good grace, perhaps vowing to keep fighting for truth, logic, and the American way.

The copyediting stage is your last chance to change the paper in any substantive way. Read it carefully, and make sure this is just what you want to say. Many journals no longer send you page proofs, so the next time you see your baby is when it appears in print in the journal. And a good day that is!

The Sticky Question of Authorship

In many fields, papers are almost exclusively written by single authors. This deftly avoids problems of authorship credit. But in many other scholarly disciplines, particularly in the natural sciences and in engineering, single-author papers are rare.[5] How to decide the order of the authors?

First the question: Does the order of names matter? *YES,* the order matters. But the order has different meanings in various fields. In many disciplines (e.g., engineering), the first author is the most important, followed by the second, and so on. The fourth author, should there be one, is almost not counted. On the other hand, in some life sciences, the last author has a position of honor because this position signifies senior leadership. The head of the laboratory in which the research was done is the last author, sort of guiding his or her underlings, unassuming and magnanimous in letting the junior people be first authors.

In large research groups, the inclusion or exclusion of a name in the list of authors can have serious consequences. For example, many laboratories employ statisticians to reduce and present the data. Should they also be listed as authors even though their only involvement in the research is doing the statistical calculations? If not, then statisticians working in laboratories would never receive credit for their work. But statisticians know little or nothing about the science in the paper and would not be able to stand behind the substance of the paper, such as presenting it to a professional audience, for example.

Another problem is whether or not to include the project officers at your funding agency, such as the National Science Foundation or the National Institutes of Health. These persons have made the research possible and were involved in its planning, but they were never in the laboratory and did not contribute any intellectual capital. Most journals now do not encourage such "honorary authors."

These are difficult questions, and each field and laboratory should decide up front what the rules are. In my own case, when I work with students on a one-on-one basis, we have a simple rule: If the student wants to publish the work as a technical paper, then he or she is the first author and I am pleased to be the second author. If the first draft has not been written within one year after graduation, then I claim ownership of the data and will publish the paper with my name first. So far I have not had any conflicts or hard feelings.

Whatever you do in your own laboratory, *make sure everyone knows what the rules are.* You can avoid hard feelings and unhappiness by making sure everyone knows up front how authorship is decided.

Writing a Book

The notion of writing a textbook is in the back of every professor's mind. After all, we are prima donnas and world experts in our chosen fields. Why should we not profess, as all good professors should, what the state of the discipline is in a book?

In the humanities and social sciences, publishing a book is a require-ment. Most universities will not consider tenure until the first book is published and the second is on the way. In the natural sciences and engineering, books are not required and might even be discouraged. In some research universities, a science textbook receives credit equivalent to one scholarly journal article. If that is the case, you should not waste your time on a textbook during your early years but rather concentrate on research publications. At other universities and colleges, however, textbooks are highly valued and count significantly in tenure and promo-tion decisions. Before you start writing, therefore, make sure the time you spend on the book is valued by those who make tenure and promo-tion decisions.

In the humanities, your first book will no doubt be your Ph.D. dissertation. Bear this in mind when you choose a dissertation topic. Remember that you have 5 or maybe 6 years to prove yourself, and writing and publishing a second book within that short time will be difficult.

Textbooks in the humanities are commonly written by a consortium of senior professors, under contract to a publisher, so it is unlikely that you will be involved in textbook publishing during the first years of your career. In the sciences and in engineering, however, the book you write will more than likely be a textbook, and it may be single-authored. You will find that if you write a good textbook and if the book is widely accepted, your career will take off. People at other universities will know of you and will pay attention to your research publications. They will recognize the hard work that has gone into the textbook and will be grateful to you for taking the time to write it.

Years ago a publisher friend of mine asked me how I wrote books. How did I decide to write a book, and how did I begin the process of writing? I thought about it a long while, because the question had never occurred to me. I thought *everyone* wanted to write books and *everyone* knew how to do it. So I replayed the process I had used in writing several textbooks.

First and foremost, I never wrote a book that I did not first teach. Once I had the course content and progression down and felt there was cohesion in presentation and substance to the course, it became a fairly simple process of transferring the course notes to a book. Teaching, therefore, became the prerequisite of writing a good textbook. I suspect that this is how all good textbooks emerge, but I have no data to prove it. I simply do not understand how it is possible to write a book without the feedback from and interaction with the students who would use the book.[6]

If you decide to turn your excellent class notes into a book, how should you proceed? You have essentially two options. First, you can sit down, bang out the manuscript, and then send it to several publishers and let them fight over it. Or you can choose one publisher and work with this publisher in the preparation of the book. The first option is risky. Suppose you have spent interminable hours on your "baby," and now everyone thinks it's ugly. Nobody wants to publish it. The second option is also difficult because you have little to convince the editor that your book will be great. This is especially true if you are a young person with no track record in publishing.

So which to do? Send in an outline or finish the book and send the entire manuscript to the publisher? If the book is not yet written, I suggest you take the safe path and not spend time finishing the manuscript until you know it will be published. There are a lot of publishers out there, and you will find one who will want to work with you. The publisher can then be a great help in the formulation of your book. If the book is your Ph.D. dissertation and it is already in good shape, clean it up and send the whole manuscript. The more information the editor, has the better informed will be the decision.

In either case, you should include a cover letter and a prospectus. A prospectus is not an abstract of your book, but rather an argument as to why your manuscript should be published. Consider both the scholarly and the financial aspects of publishing the book. The editor and the marketing department will want to publish, ideally, a scholarly best-seller. If it is a textbook, tell them how your book is different from the competition and why colleagues who teach such courses would want to use your book instead of the competition. What "hooks" can the sales department use to sell your book? If the book is unique and has no competition, the publisher will want to know who would use it—whether or not there are courses being taught that would adopt this book. If you are writing a groundbreaking book for which there are only a few courses being offered, you may have a difficult time convincing the publisher to invest in your book. In this case, explain how these courses will soon be taught at all the best universities and how your book will be the only one available.[7] If it is not a textbook, tell the editor why this field of scholarship is a hot area and how this book will fill a crucial niche in the discipline. Above all, do not be bashful. Be modestly effusive.

In contrast to professional and scholarly papers, it is perfectly all right to submit your prospectus or even entire manuscript to more than one publisher simultaneously. In your cover letter, it would be good and honest to say who else you have submitted it to. This way the publisher knows who the competition is for publishing your manuscript.

Editors of publishing houses, with a few exceptions, are not technical or scientific experts. Their knowledge of the various fields covered by the publishing house is cursory, but they are good listeners and learn a lot by talking to people who understand the field and can predict where it is going. Nevertheless, they do not trust themselves in making technical decisions and therefore have a stable of reviewers who read manuscripts or partial manuscripts to evaluate their quality. When an editor receives your manuscript or prospectus, it goes to three or more reviewers, and the decision of these anonymous reviewers is crucial in the decision to publish or not to publish. This can be frustrating to the author because some of the reviewers might not be familiar with your discipline and might not understand your book, while some may simply be incompetent. Others may have ulterior motives in panning your book. Whatever the case, the two facts are (1) editors do not trust themselves to make decisions, and (2) reviewers, as a result, have immense power in deciding whether a book is published or not.

Editors also know that reviews can be classified in two ways, shown best as a matrix:[8]

	Positive	Negative
Constructive		
Destructive		

If the editor likes the book, he or she would very much like to receive reviews that are both positive and constructive. The worst kind of review is a negative one that offers no feedback on how the book might be improved.

When the editor gets promising reviews on your manuscript, the publishing house has to decide whether or not to invest the money to publish your book. This decision involves a number of considerations, including their faith that you will finish the work. The publisher must evaluate the market for your book and decide if it can make money from publishing it.[9] Publishing yet another textbook designed for introductory psychology classes, for example, is risky because there are numerous books available for such a course; but the rewards can be staggering if the book is widely adopted.

Once the publisher decides that he or she wants to publish your book, you will be sent a contract. Royalties, for example, will be a percentage of the selling price of the book, but there will be some small print about how your royalties take a deep cut if the book sells for less than full price. Other issues might involve the number of free books the publisher will give you and at what discount you can purchase additional books. A common clause in contracts involves translations for which you and the publisher split the fee. For the most part, contracts are fairly standard and there is little to argue about. Contracts have legal value only in that you are now constrained from publishing a similar book with another publisher, and the publisher must publish your book when you have finished it. If, however, you have submitted only a few pages and an outline before the contract was agreed to, and the full manuscript turns out to be bloody awful, publishers have a way out. They can argue that you have not written the book they expected and therefore they will not publish it. You can sue them, but it isn't worth it. Similarly, if you decide to break your contract with the publisher and go for a better deal with someone else, most publishers will not bother pursuing you unless your book becomes a great financial success, at which time you will get a friendly letter from their lawyers. In short, honor thy contracts so that your days may be long in publishing.

Presenting Papers at Scholarly Conferences

All the admonitions about how to give excellent lectures apply to presenting a paper at a conference, except more so. As a young scholar, you are in great part judged by how well you can present your topic and how well you can defend against the onslaught of sometimes harsh questions.

The ordeal notwithstanding, you should make every effort as a graduate student to get on the program at quality national conferences. This exposure can be invaluable when you go looking for a job because some of the people who will be in the position of hiring you would have seen your performance at the conference.

Although every presentation is valuable because it gives you another chance to practice oratorical skills, it is important to recognize that some conferences are far more important than others, and being on the program at the best national conferences is worth many points. Seek help here from your advisor and mentor. Which conferences should you shoot for and at which would you have a reasonable chance of getting selected for a paper presentation?

If you are lucky enough to be able to present a paper to an audience, make the most of it. First do a good job, but then use the presentation to your advantage afterward. After a presentation, people will come up to you and compliment you on your presentation. "Nice talk" or "Enjoyed it." Thank them for the kind words, but then take it further. Ask them about the significance of the work relative to their own research, or ask them how you might improve it, or how you should extend the topic further. Great ideas can come from such informal conversations. And make sure you exchange business cards.

Over the past few decades, science and engineering conferences have developed the idea of *poster sessions* to provide a forum for those researchers whose papers are not judged appropriate for oral presentations. Poster sessions involve setting up a series of posters on a board, generally 3 feet by 4 feet, that summarize your research. During the poster sessions, the authors stand by their posters and wait for interested onlookers to wander by.

The beauty of these sessions is that if you are interested in a specific research topic, you can meet and talk with the author, asking questions and getting clarification on difficult points. Thus, the interested "reader" can get a lot of information on specific topics in poster sessions. The author, however, is exposed to only a few passersby and cannot get the publicity he or she believes is deserving of the research. Nevertheless, if the opportunity arises, presenting a poster at a major conference is a great opportunity for young researchers looking for employment, because the potential employers will pay close attention to how you present the material and how you respond to questions.

Notes

1. Astin, A. W., Korn, W. S., & Day, E. L. (1991). *The American college teacher: National norms for the 1989-1990 HERI faculty survey.* Los Angeles: Higher Education Research Institute.

2. Bedeian, A. (1996). Lessons learned along the way: Twelve suggestions for optimizing career success. In P. J. Frost & M. S. Taylor (Eds.), *Rhythms of academic life* (p. 15). Thousand Oaks, CA: Sage.

3. The worst case of editorial abuse I know of is the journal editor who would recommend publishing a paper in his own field only if his own name was added to the list of authors.

4. Meyer, A. D. (1996). Balls, strikes and collisions on the base path: Ruminations of a veteran reviewer. In P. J. Frost & M. S. Taylor (Eds.), *Rhythms of academic life* (p. 280). Thousand Oaks, CA: Sage.

5. This is not to say that the natural sciences and engineering do not value single-author papers. As discussed in the chapter on tenure, you should strive to have at least a few papers with you as the single author, thus demonstrating independence from your mentor and other hangers-on.

6. This book is no exception. I have been teaching a course for a number of years to Duke University School of Engineering senior graduate students interested in pursuing academic careers, and this book is the result.

7. In 1970, for example, I wrote a book on environmental pollution and control and sent it to numerous publishers. No one wanted to publish it because there were no such courses. Finally, a small publisher decided to risk it. The book is still in print, in its fifth edition. The courses simply came to the book.

8. Thanks to Harry Briggs, Sage Publications.

9. This includes not-for-profit university presses. Their mission statements often speak to the publishing of high-quality scholarship regardless of how many copies the book would sell, but this is only partly true. University presses must be essentially self-supporting and must make money to stay in business.

CHAPTER 11

Getting
Tenure

Free inquiry demands free thinking and free speech. The university can survive as a place of learning and intellectual development only by allowing the faculty to tell the truth as they understand it. Universities must allow faculty the right to express their opinions on substantive issues without censorship.

Big deal. Don't we already have free speech in the United States? The First Amendment to the United States Constitution guarantees free speech, doesn't it?

No, not really. The First Amendment prohibits *government* reprisal for saying what is on our mind. This amendment does not cover *private* organizations such as churches, companies, or universities. A disagreement in theology can get a preacher fired. An honest but negative evaluation of a product's usefulness can end an executive's career in a corporation. In fact, the university is the only institution that guarantees its employees the right to express their opinions without threat of reprisal from the institution. Such academic freedom is a hard-won right and is jealously guarded by the professorate.

Academic freedom is not license to do or say anything you want. But academic freedom does protect you from getting fired for saying things that might be unpopular with the administration or politicians who, at least in the case of public universities, have the final say in university affairs. Academic freedom, so the argument goes, is possible only if the university cannot fire you for speaking out on issues of importance and for speaking the truth as you see it. The contract between faculty and university must, therefore, contain a "no fire" clause. This is called *tenure*.

Not all colleges and universities yield full academic freedom to its faculties. Church-supported schools can often demand that the faculty adhere to a set of religious beliefs and can fire faculty for expressing contrary views. In recent years, hurtful speech, especially about race and gender, has been the cause for dismissal (see Chapter 13 on how to lose a tenured job). We must conclude, therefore, that tenure is a tenuous concept and that there really is no such thing as free speech in a university. Why then do we have tenure, and why do universities and faculty both defend it?

The Origins and Justification for Tenure

Academic freedom is not an inalienable right. During the 19th century, little academic freedom existed in American universities. Firing faculty for speaking out on issues such as slavery or Darwinism was common. Most universities were governed by boards of trustees who had little patience with people who did not believe the way they did.

During the beginning of the 20th century, the notion of academic freedom began to seep into universities and several cases became famous, not the least of which was the Bassett affair at Trinity College, a Methodist-supported teachers college (now Duke University) in segregationist North Carolina.

In 1900, John Spencer Bassett was a 36-year-old English professor at Trinity College. Although he was born and raised in eastern North Carolina, he believed that segregationist politicians in the South exploited the race issue for political gain and that the disfranchisement of blacks hurt the progress of the South. He called for a spirit of reconciliation between the races in the literary journal *South Atlantic Quarterly*. The most famous phrase out of the article, which his critics used unmercifully against him, was the claim that "[Booker T.] Washington is a great man . . . and take him all in all the greatest man, save General Lee, born in the South in a hundred years. . . ."

The establishment reaction was swift and vicious. Josephus Daniels, the powerful Democratic editor of the Raleigh *News and Observer,* thundered in editorials against Bassett, calling for his dismissal. Most newspapers in North Carolina soon joined the chorus. The businessmen and Methodist ministers who made up the Trinity College board of trustees faced immense pressure to fire Bassett.

Fortunately, the president of Trinity College was John Kilgo, a Methodist minister and fighter for social causes. He rallied the faculty and students at Trinity College and convinced several influential trustees such as Benjamin Duke that academic freedom deserved protection. In a fateful meeting of the board of trustees, the vote was 18 to 7 to support Bassett. This decision made national news and boosted the reputation of Trinity College.[1] The affair set a precedent for other universities and made academic freedom a core value in university life.

But not all academic freedom cases were as clear-cut or resulted in similar action. In 1899, Emory College in Atlanta dismissed a professor who published an article in the *Atlantic Monthly* attacking the brutality of whites against blacks. In 1900 at Stanford University, Professor Edward Ross was fired from the faculty ostensibly for his outspoken and unorthodox views on economics. Ross was a distinguished economist who supported William Jennings Bryant and the Free Silver Movement. Jane Stanford, chair of the board of trustees, asked President David Starr Jordan to fire Ross, and eventually the president did so. It was well-known that Jane Stanford was opposed to the populist views of Ross, and it was assumed that this was the cause for the firing. What is not so widely known is that Ross had also made some incredibly insensitive racist remarks about Asian immigration, at a time when Stanford was trying to provide educational opportunities for Asian immigrants. Possibly the firing was more for the "hate speech" than for his economic views.[2]

Tenure as we now know it was originally established at the University of Wisconsin in the early 1900s. Wisconsin was a hotbed of progressive ideas, and professors speaking radical thoughts believed they needed the protection of the university. The fledgling American Association of University Professors (AAUP), formed in 1915 by a number of prominent faculty from 60 institutions, quickly became involved in the defense of academic freedom. Its first published work was the 1915 Declaration of its Committee on Academic Freedom and Tenure. In the 1940s the AAUP, the closest organization university faculty have to a union,[3] promulgated a set of guidelines that defined what tenure at universities is to mean. This AAUP document is still the operative statement on tenure and is respected by most universities even though the document has no legal standing.

Competitive pressures for hiring the best professors caused most universities to accept the AAUP definition voluntarily and adopt a system for tenuring faculty, a system that has changed little over the past 60 years. Basically, the university agrees to provide a lifetime job for the faculty as long as the members adhere to a code of conduct that includes doing their job (teaching classes) and being morally upright. Morality used to mean exclusively sexual morality, but in the last few years professors have lost their jobs for committing petty crimes. Universities actually have a number of ways of dismissing tenured professors, the most drastic being simply declaring that all tenure is revoked and cleaning house, as was the case recently at Bennington College. Tenure, therefore, should not be thought of as a lifetime contract as much as it is a simple agreement of goodwill between the faculty and the university.

The Tenuring Process

While details of the process vary from university to university, the essential elements are the same. Although tenure can be awarded as a recruitment tool for senior faculty who have proven records of accomplishment, in this discussion I focus exclusively on the tenuring process for junior faculty who are hired as assistant professors.

Depending on the contract, the tenure review process can be initiated at any time, typically 5 or 6 years after the initial appointment. If the contract is for 7 years, the review takes place during the 6th year, and the decision is made at the end of that year. If you try for tenure during your 6th year and the decision is negative, you will have one more year left on your contract to find another job. In effect this means that you really have only five years to prove yourself worthy of tenure before the material presented for review is compiled.

The tenure clock is stopped at most institutions when women take time out to have children. For example, at the University of Maryland, the policy states that in recognition of the effects that pregnancy, childbirth, and related medical conditions can have upon the time and energy a woman has to devote to her professional responsibilities, thus on her ability to work at the pace or level expected to achieve tenure, a woman who bears one or more children during her probationary period shall, upon written request . . . be granted an exclusion of one year from the countable years of service that constitute such tenure probationary period.

If you are a woman and you are counting on starting or expanding your family during the probationary years of the tenure process, you should most certainly find out about the policy at the university. But given the residual chauvinism toward women, it probably would not be a good idea to discuss this at the initial interview stage.

The tenuring process begins when the department chair appoints an ad hoc committee, usually consisting of three tenured faculty members whose duty it is to assemble the *dossier*. The dossier is a compilation of the candidate's performance, including the résumé, copies of publications, letters of recommendation, and other material. The chair of the ad hoc committee and the candidate should be on good terms, because the quality of the dossier is very important, and the committee can significantly influence that quality. The chair of the ad hoc committee gathers all the necessary information from the candidate, including a current résumé, a statement indicating directions of future scholarly work and intellectual development, copies of key papers and other publications, a statement on the quality of the journals in which the papers appeared, representative course outlines, students' teaching evaluations, and recent grant proposals.

The most important function of the ad hoc committee is to solicit letters of recommendation and evaluation from scholars outside the university. Typically the committee chair asks the candidate to provide some names, while the committee and/or the departmental chair selects other outside evaluators.

The selection of these names is a critical part of the tenure game. And strangely enough, you the candidate should not select the persons who you would consider your strongest references. The provost's review committee will discount the opinions of any person suggested by the candidate, regardless of how renowned the evaluator may be, because they recognize that the candidate would of course select only those people whom he or she knows would write good letters. Letters from the dissertation advisor or any other scholars from the university from which you have received your degrees are especially worthless.

The obvious ploy here is therefore for you to not recommend any names. Or, better yet, if the departmental chair is sympathetic and willing, the candidate can tell the chair who should be contacted, but the chair makes the official recommendation of reviewers to the ad hoc committee. Above all, you should not "use up" good evaluators by proposing them directly to the ad hoc committee. Because letters from Ph.D. advisors are ignored, it makes sense to recommend only your advisor(s).

The external evaluators receive a package that contains the résumé, intellectual statement, and typically the most important publications. The letter usually asks specific questions, one of which is often, "Would the candidate receive tenure at your university?" Because of elitism in academia, the university where the evaluators work is very important. A response from Yale or Princeton or Stanford or Caltech that, yes, this person would probably receive tenure, is an extremely strong recommendation. The same response from a local teachers college is basically worthless. On the other hand, a negative response from the teachers college is deadly. It makes sense to ask only professors at top universities for outside evaluations. Equally important are the positions or titles of the evaluators. For maximum effect, they should all be named professors at prestigious universities, or department chairs or deans at major universities. A few Nobel laureates would also help, of course.

The choice of who gets to be an evaluator is crucial in the tenure process. If the ad hoc committee, and particularly its chair, are either unsympathetic or even antagonistic, the process can for all intents and purposes be killed at the letter-writing stage. Only one negative letter from an eminent evaluator can easily kill a tenure case.

Outside evaluators are especially important because few, if any, of the people who make the final decision are experts in the candidate's field of research. The opinions of scholars *outside* the university matter a great deal more than the opinions of scholars within the university. What this does is to fractionate the university. To get tenure, young scholars must impress people outside the university and concentrate their efforts on building a reputation within some narrow field, ignoring (safely) responsibilities within the university from which they get their paycheck. It appears that the university is the only institution that allows its competitors to decide who will be retained and promoted. Imagine Ford Motor Company asking General Motors to choose its engineers and managers.

After all the letters of evaluation have been received, the ad hoc committee assembles the dossier, which by this time is so large that it requires a box. Based on all this information, the ad hoc committee writes a letter to the departmental chair summarizing the information and making a recommendation. This letter and the entire dossier now go to the tenured members of the department, who meet to consider the next step—to recommend or not recommend tenure. Faculty take these votes seriously. Secret paper ballots are used. Even then, strong and emotional battles can rage over a particular case, often widening existing schisms within the department. Few will be convinced by facts once their minds are made up. Regardless of the vote, the departmental chair then writes a letter to the dean reporting the departmental vote and summarizing the discussions by the faculty. The letter concludes with the chair's own recommendation to the dean.

Now the entire dossier, with the chair's letter, goes to the dean, who has an opportunity to comment and recommend action. In most cases, the dean cannot formally stop the process, but if the case is very weak and the faculty and the departmental chair have not recommended tenure, the dean will suggest that the candidate withdraw the application for tenure.

If the dean's evaluation is favorable, the dean adds a letter to the dossier, and the whole works goes to the provost or vice president for academic affairs, who usually has an advisory committee for evaluating all university tenure cases. Often this committee is the most difficult to convince, partly because most of the members typically do not understand or appreciate the candidate's area of expertise and partly because they might work under the illogical notion that they are doing their job only if they refuse tenure in a certain fraction of cases.

Universities are understandably careful about giving tenure to too many faculty and the provost's committee is the place where these quotas are implemented. If a department has a high fraction of tenured faculty, it becomes much less likely that a young professor in that department will receive tenure. Some universities will assign tenure slots to departments, and a young faculty member would be hired with the understanding that such a slot will be reserved for him or her.

Most members of the provost's committee are ignorant of the candidate's field of expertise, and yet must make a decision on his or her qualifications. For a scientist or engineer, a knowledgeable decision based on the contribution to the candidate's discipline cannot be made by the art historians and sociologists on the provost's committee, and vice versa. These evaluators must rely on the outside letters, or they may even contact acquaintances at other universities, seeking guidance. Such contacts are both unethical and dangerous, because nobody outside the provost's committee knows about them and because such flimsy evidence is a poor foundation for a decision.

Often the provost's committee, in an admirable but dangerous attempt to obtain additional information, will ask the dean or the departmental chair to visit with them. While such an interview is not quite an inquisition in the worst sense, it is a difficult situation for the chair or the dean. He or she is placed on the spot in having to defend the evaluations. Often the provost's committee will ask one question: "Could we get someone else better than this candidate for this position?" The departmental chair can torpedo the candidate at this point simply by answering affirmatively. The case is closed and tenure is denied, regardless of the actual quality of the applicant. All such conversations are off the record, and there is no appeal.

This system gives immense power to the departmental chair. Sadly, the chair may be ignorant of the details of the candidate's discipline or may have personal reasons for disliking the candidate. No matter. The provost's ad hoc committee does not know this. Young faculty must therefore recognize this problem. If they perceive that they cannot obtain a favorable evaluation from the chair, they ought to consider alternative employment.

One way or another, the provost's committee then makes a recommendation to the provost, who in turn makes the final decision. Provosts who value the advice of their advisory committees will not go against their recommendation too often, and usually the vote of the committee is the final decision.

Formality dictates that tenure is not final until the board of trustees approves the nomination. Although the board of trustees is supposed to be the court of last appeal for unfair decisions, they seldom vote against the provost. Such a move would be a vote of no confidence, and the university would soon be looking for a new provost.

Most universities have an appeals process, but only for procedural appeals. Without procedural error, there is little that can be done to reverse a negative decision. Some faculty have sued in courts of law but never with success (except in cases of procedural errors or discrimination). Court cases fail because the information is confidential. The candidate will never, for example, see the external letters of evaluation. If one or more of these letters is negative, the candidate cannot refute the facts because he or she is never allowed to see the letter or even know who sent the letter.

Because of the "up or out" nature of the tenure process, you might be encouraged to initiate the tenure process earlier than the sixth year with the argument that if you are turned down you will have another opportunity to try again. This is a tricky question and the decision depends on many variables:

• Is the chair of the department a strong supporter or not, and when will he or she be stepping down? If the chair is a strong supporter and you are uncertain of the new chair's enthusiasm for your tenure, it might be wise to try early.

• What is the trajectory of your accomplishments? If you have just received an NSF Career Award (a very prestigious grant) and you have just published 10 papers last year, this might be a good time to try for it. Next year might not be so impressive.

• How many other assistant professors are in line for the tenure process? If waiting for your full probationary time means that you will be going up with several other assistant professors from your department, then it might be wise to try to stagger the applications. A good departmental chair will recognize this and advise you accordingly.

• If at your university the real bottleneck is with the provost's advisory committee, you may not want to send your dossier back to the same group who turned you down once. They will remember all the reasons why they did not agree to tenure in the first place and will be less likely to grant it this time around unless you have had a phenomenally productive year.

Most important is to talk this over with the chair of your department and plan your strategy. Most chairs will be strong supporters and will not torpedo you.

An Alternative Path to Tenure

There is an alternative path to tenure. You do not have to start as an assistant professor and compete with all of your peers for the few tenured slots that the university might be willing to offer. You will be dreadfully busy the first few years with your teaching responsibilities and will have little time left for your scholarly activity. Your heart will be in the classroom, but your tenure will be judged on the basis of grants secured and research results produced. And at the end of 7 years, if you have not made the grade, you will be fired because of the system set up by the AAUP, the same organization that purports to be the great protector of the professorate.

The alternative route to tenure is to enter a governmental or private research organization upon graduation, or if you are in the humanities, some organizations such as the Department of Defense or the Brookings Institution that hires historians, economists, and other educated people. In such organizations, your tasks will be greatly simplified and your job description will be much simpler and clearer. You will work an 8-hour day and have time off. You will have a fund for travel, and you will have collegial and helpful support staff. The research and scholarship you do will be practical and useful and will be judged on the basis of your skills as a researcher and scholar.

The major caveat with this route to tenure is that you may find yourself in an organization where you will not be free to publish everything you discover. Before signing on to a nonacademic organization, and if you still desire to eventually become a professor, you *must* have an understanding about full publication.

If then all goes well, 7 or 8 years have passed, your résumé is bulging with scholarly papers published and discoveries made, and you have established yourself as a force in the discipline, you can apply to universities to enter the professorate as an associate professor with tenure.

Is There Life After a Negative Tenure Decision?

Yes, there is life after being rejected for tenure. The world does not end with a negative tenure decision, even though you might feel that all your efforts and sacrifice have gone to waste. With one decision, your academic career has ended.

But not so fast. Often other universities and colleges are on the lookout for good people who have been badly treated, and you can find a satisfying job at another school. Recently a scientist at Duke was refused tenure and the next year found a full (tenured) professorship at Yale. The negative decision also opens up new career possibilities that you may not have considered, or it allows you to get into private practice where you can use your skills and learn new ones for an eventual reentry into academia. Many excellent and satisfied academicians today have been the recipients of negative tenure decisions and have learned from the experience and become better professors as a result. So there is life after a negative tenure decision, although the first few days after the crushing blow may not seem to hold any hope for the future.

The fact remains that as a young professor your academic future is judged on a few years of work at the start of your career. You might be an enthusiastic, valuable, and loyal faculty member and then you are in effect fired, often suspending or even truncating a promising academic career. Is this fair to the individual, and is this the best system we can have for developing a strong faculty?

Arguments Against Tenure

Three arguments are commonly presented against tenure. The first argument against tenure is that it does not accomplish its aims—to guarantee academic freedom. The AAUP claims that the absence of tenure will create chaos in academia, and yet we have institutions where the rights of faculty are strictly limited on religious or other grounds, while other institutions have either abolished or severely curtailed tenure with no apparent ill effects. In support of this argument, note that all of our untenured faculty members do not, by definition, have the protection of tenure and many of them are socially and politically active. Although the data would be impossible to obtain, I doubt if a single nontenured faculty member has been dismissed in the past 50 years for making unpopular social or political statements. The coupling of academic freedom with tenure is therefore inappropriate. In today's social climate, there is no clear cause and effect. Academic freedom does not exist because of the tenure system.

The second argument against tenure is that it does not produce the best faculty. There is no doubt that some of our best teachers are denied tenure because they are not sufficiently productive in research or scholarship. For recent Ph.D. graduates the thought of up-or-out tenure decisions is not an inducement when they are seeking their first jobs. Many graduate students are pleased to find that some universities do not have strict tenure policies or that nontenure track appointments are possible. These students have a sense of their own worth and would want to prove their value to the university unencumbered by the tenure decision. They shy away from universities that have strict tenure policies and a poor record of retainment. Tenure is therefore unlikely to enhance the quality of an academic institution.

Finally, tenure is and has been used by lazy or unethical senior faculty to provide a secure income while they pursue outside interests. While some outside work can be useful if brought to the classroom or research laboratory, often the interests have little to do with their scholarly field. One senior professor at the University of North Carolina, for example, runs a funeral home and comes to the university only once a week to teach a small seminar that has not changed in 20 years, all the time drawing a full professor's salary.

Arguments against tenure have gained steam in the past few years. For example, the author of one paper argues that

> tenure has nearly the opposite effects on professors than are typically claimed for it: Tenure is inimical to academic freedom; it discourages radical innovation and risk taking; it limits the mobility of professors; and it may even work to the ultimate advantage of administrators in bargaining with professors.[4]

Why, then, does tenure exist? I believe there are three reasons. First, I believe that many faculty deeply and firmly believe that academic tenure is absolutely necessary to retain their academic freedom. De George, in his book supporting tenure, states flatly that "the justification [for tenure] is that academic tenure is the best means our society has devised to secure and preserve academic freedom."[5]

Without doubt, academic freedom is important to society because the free university is the place where truth is to be discovered. If academic tenure is the best way to preserve academic freedom, then academic tenure is good for society and should be preserved.

But this argument takes a huge jump in logic. If we agree that academic freedom is good for society and should be preserved, how can we show that the present tenure system is the only way we can guarantee academic freedom? We can prove that this is not causal by proving either that such a relationship does not exist or that there can be other equally feasible solutions. We cannot do the former, but is it possible to show that academic freedom can be preserved and guaranteed by means other than tenure? Of course. For example, take the situation where all faculty have civil service jobs (as is the case in many countries such as Canada) and firing civil service employees is notoriously difficult. Civil service employees are protected by the First Amendment to the Bill of Rights, guaranteeing free speech. This amendment says that the government (the employer in this case) cannot prevent people from speaking their mind, and thus academic freedom would be guaranteed. I am not advocating that all faculty become civil servants, but I am showing, I hope, that De George's argument for the retention of tenure in universities is a hollow one.

The second reason tenure still exists is that universities that competitively recruit faculty and administrators believe that not being able to offer tenure to senior faculty would place them at a disadvantage. Tenure, if it is ever to be abolished, has to be abolished by agreement between enough universities to make it irrelevant as a recruitment tool.

The third reason tenure exists is that some senior faculty, who have long ceased to be productive, hold on to their jobs by virtue of the "no fire" clause. They realize that the elimination of tenure will expose them to comparison with other faculty and that this might result in their dismissal. These faculty, therefore, fight the hardest to retain the system.

Will the tenure system ever be changed? Yes, in my opinion, and the change will come from the outside—from the politicians for state universities and from the boards of trustees at the private universities who will ask tough questions and get wobbly answers from supporters of the present system. If you are just beginning your academic career, you can expect to see huge changes in the tenure system during your lifetime.

Perhaps, with luck, you will even be instrumental in promoting and facilitating the best of these long overdue changes.

Notes

1. For an excellent discussion of the Bassett affair, see Durden, R. R. (1975). *The Dukes of Durham*. Durham, NC: Duke University Press.

2. Kennedy, D. (1997). *Academic duty* (p. 124). Cambridge, MA: Harvard University Press.

3. Some faculty have, of course, joined unions, but these are existing unions that represent many trades. There is no "Amalgamated Professors Union" or such.

4. Adela, J. (1994). Tenure, a conscientious objection. *Change* (May/June), 29.

5. De George, R. T. (1997). *Academic freedom and tenure* (p. 9). Lanham, MD: Rowan & Littlefield.

CHAPTER 12

Academic Integrity

Some senior teachers are fond of referring to the *teachable moment,* or that instant when the student is ready to absorb some kernel of knowledge. Unhappily, such teachable moments do not come all that often, but the occasional ones provide a feeling of satisfaction comparable to a perfect chip shot to the green.

Often such teachable moments do not come in the classroom but during incidental contact with students. In one case, I was speaking to a particularly obnoxious undergraduate in my office concerning a minor ethical violation. He decided to challenge me and asked with a smirk, "Why *shouldn't* I cheat?"

I recognized the teachable moment, but I was not fully prepared to answer him. His is a difficult question, actually. He could have made a strong case for cheating. If grades are so important, then all he is doing is increasing his grade point average. He would still learn as much as he would without cheating, but he gets higher grades. So why should he not cheat all he can as long as he does not get caught? This is a competitive world, and he is only doing what is best for him personally.

As a young professor, you will have few problems more difficult than coping with academic integrity. Invariably some bad will result from cheating. Either the student, or you, or the school, or all will suffer. In this chapter, I first talk about the moral justification for maintaining an atmosphere of honor within an academic community, followed by some suggestions for preventing breaches of conduct. Finally, I discuss another kind of academic integrity, the problem of fraud, plagiarism, and conflict of interest by professors.

Moral Justification
for Academic Honor

The two philosophical questions that require answers are (1) Why should cheating be prohibited? and (2) Why should I not cheat? The burden of proof is on us to convince students not only that cheating should not be condoned, but that there are good arguments for why they should not cheat.

First, we have a number of strong arguments to convince the student that cheating should be prohibited. On a moral level, cheating can be thought of as stealing. Every time a student cheats, he or she devalues the work of other students. Even if the grades are not on a curve, the cheater's A grade makes the other A grades less valuable. This is simply stealing from others.

Another approach is to argue that we have a common responsibility to maintain a civil society. We make rules for how to behave toward each other. Some of these rules are so important that we codify them into laws. It is illegal, for example, to drive on the wrong side of the street. But other rules are informal and exist only because we know that disobeying these rules would lead to a society where none of us wants to live. Suppose there were no (unspoken) rules on how to drive a shopping cart in the supermarket. It would be a free-for-all with people pushing and shoving each other at the checkout counter. The strongest would prevail and the weaker would suffer. None of us wants to live in such a society, and we recognize that courtesy and etiquette are essential to civilization.

The same is true with academic integrity. Few would consider cheating an option at schools where it just "is not done." At such schools, the students value the system most ardently and treat offenders harshly. But where an atmosphere and tradition of honor do not exist, academic anarchy can prevail. There are colleges in the United States where almost everyone cheats, and the faculty or the administration does nothing about it. I can't imagine working in such a place, and I am sure the students would want the situation to be different as well. Recently the students at Howard University staged a protest to express their concern that the administration was not taking cheating seriously enough. Most students at most universities understand and care about academic integrity, and the reason to not condone cheating is simply to maintain a system that is a good system—one that is fair and just and that allows the people who work the hardest to succeed.

But now to the more difficult question of why students as individuals should not cheat. There are two approaches to answering this question. The first task is to appeal to their own well-being and happiness, and to suggest that cheating is not to their benefit. For example, on the crudest level, no student wants to suffer the shame, humiliation, and financial hardship (not to mention the parental guilt trip) should they get caught. This argument might work for some students, but not all. Most students who cheat believe that they will escape detection. Punishment as deterrence only has marginal value.

A second argument for students who intend not to get caught is that in cheating they will diminish their own self-worth. Sissela Bok, in her excellent book *Lying,* argues that people should not lie under most circumstances but acknowledges that there might be situations where telling a lie is morally obligatory (such as a lie to save an innocent life).[1] But every time one tells a lie, whatever the reason, one loses some personal dignity. One is simply less of a person for having told a lie. The same is true of cheating. Cheating and getting away with it has a hidden personal cost. Knowing you have obtained something (such as a college degree) not by hard work but by cheating diminishes its value in your own eyes. It will never be the source of pride it could otherwise be.

A third approach to promote honesty is to argue that each student is part of a greater community—the university. The success of the institution depends on maintaining the integrity and honesty of its individual parts. Students are integral to the academic enterprise and good academic citizens do not cheat.

Finally, the argument based on moral values—that cheating is simply wrong—is a powerful argument for many. As we grow and mature, we all develop our patterns and concepts of moral values. We begin to believe that some things are right (truth, honesty, justice) and some things are wrong (hurting others, lying, breaking promises), and we develop our own moral compass. We do not always *do* what we know is right, but we begin to *know* the difference between right and wrong. In short, we develop a conscience. How this happens is still a mystery, and why it happens in some to a deeper and more sensitive level than in others is unknown. But no human is without it. It is this conscience that we can appeal to in the final analysis to convince the student not to cheat. Cheating is just simply *wrong*.

Preventing Cheating

Some schools have very strong and vigorous honor systems, such as Macalester College or Haverford College, where cheating is not tolerated. Students monitor themselves and punish the offenders. There is, of course, a self-selection involved here. The kinds of students who choose to go to Macalester or Haverford buy into the system up front. Students who might cheat elsewhere are less likely to do so in a more vigilant community. Establishing such a society is hard work and cannot be achieved quickly. Often universities believe that simply establishing an honor code for the students will help solve the cheating problem. Unfortunately, it is the ambiance of the place that must be changed, and the honor code is simply the first step. What has to follow is a concerted and steady effort to enforce and promote the honor code.

Let us assume that you have taken a job in a typical university that might or might not have an honor code. Studies have shown that in such typical universities, 75% of the students have cheated at least once during their time there, and 25% of the students are habitual cheaters.[2] Remember these statistics when you start your job. Do not just assume that your students are ladies and gentlemen who would never even think of cheating. There is nothing wrong with treating them as ladies and gentlemen, but your first responsibility is to minimize temptations.

The most important rule of deterrence is to treat students with respect and to let them know what the rules are and what your position is. If you believe that students should work together on homework assignments, then you have to tell them this and write it on the course syllabus. If you want them to do their own work and not even talk to each other about the assignments, make this clear on the syllabus and discuss it during the first class meeting. At exam time, remind them of the honor code and your serious intention to make it work. Have them sign the honor pledge at the conclusion of the examination. Much can be gained by such forthrightness. Students not only are deterred from doing wrong but will respect you for your principles.

Often there are little things you can do to prevent abuse of the honor system. For example:

Blue books. If you use blue books in an examination, buy them yourself, or if the students bring them to class, collect them as the entrance "ticket" and then distribute them to the students, thus preventing some pretest writing. Do not allow them to remove pages from the books on which they may have written notes.

Seating. Spread the students out so that it is difficult to look at each other's paper during the exam. Assign seating so that students who might want to collaborate during an exam will not be able to sit together.

Exams. Give exams in which cheating is difficult. Do not use multiple- choice or true-and-false tests, but ask for short answers or essays. Don't ever ask students to memorize equations or conversion factors or lists. For example, a bad question that encourages cheating might be:

1. Using the Darcy-Weisbach equation for pressure drop, calculate the loss in pressure for a 100 m long and 5 cm diameter cast iron line with a flow of $0.1 m^3$/sec.

This requires the student to memorize the Darcy-Weisbach equation, a totally worthless exercise. Engineers should be able to look these equations up and know how to do the calculations once they have found the equation. Far better would be to give the students the equations and ask them to use the equations to solve problems.

Another bad question might be:

2. List the 20 species of trees beavers prefer for building their dams.

If students know that you ask for such lists, they will be tempted to write them on personal items or body parts or store them in programmable calculators. And anyway, why should students be able to list the species of trees? Asking them to memorize such trivia is not education. Far better to ask them to write about the structural elements of the beaver dam, or even discuss the ethical problems of controlling beaver populations.

Removing temptations. Do not place students in the position of having to juggle two primary moral values, such as academic integrity and loyalty to a friend. Suppose you give a test in one period and give the same test the next period to another class. The implied promise students make to you is that they will not tell the students in the second class what is on the test. But they might also cheat for the sake of friendship. It is unwise and unfair to place them in such situations. Give two different tests and normalize the scores.

In most lower-level courses, choose the paper topics for them to write on, and give them a short time to write the paper. Suppose you are teaching an introductory ethics class, and you have covered utilitarianism and epicurean philosophy. Give them 2 days to write a paper contrasting how the two ethical theories might resolve a particular social problem. The 2 days is much too short for them to start reading the required material. They would have already had to read the material, and then spend the next 2 days writing a response to the question, and, if the topic is sufficiently specific, they would not be able to purchase a term paper from the ubiquitous supplier. It would be difficult to cheat on such term paper assignments. Open paper topics should be reserved for upper-level courses and seminars where the selection of the topic becomes part of the assignment.[3]

Vigilance. A common form of cheating for science and engineering students is to change the answers on a returned exam and submit the correct answers for regrading, claiming that the grader did not see the problem solved correctly. You can deter this by announcing that you will randomly photocopy examinations before they are handed back. Whether or not you actually do that is not so important. The mere threat will deter this form of cheating.

Using the Judicial System

Every college and university has a judicial system to deal with breaches of academic integrity. These can vary from autocratic "star chambers" with only faculty and administrators to student-run judicial boards with members elected by the student body. In all cases, strict rules and penalties govern transgressions, including procedures specifying the appeals process. More often that not, the judicial system attempts to balance the rights of the accused with the need of the institution to maintain integrity.

The major question for you, as a faculty member, is whether or not you should use the system. When you discover a breach of integrity, you have to make a conscious choice of whether to ignore the incident, handle the situation yourself, or take it to the judicial board. How to make that decision?

First, you have to have evidence. You cannot confront the student or go to the board with mere suspicions, any more than you can go to any court of law with suspicions. You have to have the goods on the offender.

Suppose you did photocopy examinations from two students (perhaps having had some suspicions beforehand), and you have in your hand the two copies. Knockdown evidence. But this is a rare case. Often you have a far murkier situation such as a plagiarized paper in which the student has altered just enough to make it questionable.

In either case, do you have a moral obligation to do anything? Of course! Just as students have a moral obligation not to cheat, you have a moral obligation to the university to prevent the deterioration of academic integrity. You would be letting down the entire enterprise if you did not take action. But what action?

You can handle this on a personal level using frontier justice, by giving the student an F grade on the examination, or even an F grade for the course. But this alternative is wrong in two respects. First is the question of fairness. In similar situations in other courses, what would be the proper punishment? You do not know this. By applying your own punishment, you are placing the student in a position of being able to appeal (with some justification) on the basis of arbitrary and discriminatory punishment.

Second, you want the university to be on your side. Students (and their parents, and increasingly the parents' lawyers) come up with all kinds of reasons why you treated the student unfairly, and they may sue you personally in a court of law. If this happens, you are placed on the defensive, and if you have handled the situation yourself without going through the proper channels, *the university will not back you up*. This now becomes a civil case between you and the student, and the university counsel will not want to be involved. You are left hanging out there, slowly twisting in the wind. Not a pretty picture.

The smartest thing for you to do when in possession of incontrovertible evidence of cheating is to go through the judicial system. Yes, it will take time, and, yes, they might let the rascal off. But the process tries to be fair to everyone, and you now enjoy the full legal backing of the institution.

Honor in Research and Publishing

When we were kids, we all made up games to play. The rules of a game often evolved, but there was always an agreement as to how the game was played, and there was no compulsion to cheat because cheating destroyed the game. If we were playing hide-and-seek and agreed that some area was out of bounds, then hiding there would have stopped the game. We enjoyed the game more than we enjoyed winning by underhanded means and therefore agreed to abide by our rules.

The rules for more complex and organized games are of two kinds—formal rules and those rules that are simply understood to be part of the game. In bridge, for example, following suit is a written rule, while the peeking at your neighbor's cards, even if they are visible to you, is simply not done. The violation of either a written or unwritten rule may result in alienation and possible exclusion from the game. In baseball, trying to score by running over the catcher is within the formal rules, but this action is not considered appropriate in an all-star game where unnecessary injury could cost a career. When Pete Rose did exactly that, he was roundly criticized for unnecessary roughness. A player who truly values the game would not have done it.

In many ways, an academic career is a game with its share of cooperation and competition. Like all games, academia has many written and unwritten rules. The rules differ somewhat between the sciences and the humanities, but in both cases, the essence of academic integrity boils down to *truthfulness*.

When a scientist needs information on any technical or scientific topic, he or she goes to the library and looks it up. In so doing, the scientist assumes that the material in print is true and based on actual experimental evidence. If the interest is in a chemical procedure to synthesize an organic compound and a procedure for doing this is found in the literature, there is a reasonable expectation that this procedure will work and that the published material is based on actual laboratory experience. There is the assumption that only truth reaches print.

This is not a bad assumption. The scientific and technical establishment has created a filter through which all published material must pass before it sees print. First, most laboratories and other research establishments have an internal check and do not allow a paper based on questionable science to leave the laboratory. The organization of the laboratories, including the managerial control by the laboratory director, should prevent the preparation of papers not meeting the truthfulness criteria. More important, the papers undergo peer review before publication, and the more prestigious the journal, the harsher the review. Reviewers catch most of the errors and misrepresentations. Finally, once the papers are published, interested researchers in other laboratories may duplicate the procedures and confirm the results. In looking for technical material in the journals, therefore, you have some genuine assurance that the papers you are reading are believable and that the authors themselves actually did obtain all the data reported.

One of the problems in the sciences that can lead to problems is data reduction and the statistical meaning of "significance." Convention dictates that results of experimental studies are assumed persuasive (and policy decisions are made on the basis of these results) when the level of significance is less than 0.05—that is, when it is statistically likely that the result obtained would have been possible only in less than 1 in 20 chances. The success or failure of major studies revolves around the level of significance obtained.

Suppose a new drug is to be tested, and an experiment is designed where the drug is to be given to 40 patients and a placebo is given to 40 ideally identical patients. After some time, the number of people still with the disease is compared with the number of those who have been cured. Suppose, of the 40 that were given the new drug, 29 were cured and 11 were not cured. Of the ones given the placebo, 20 got better and 20 still had the disease. This is a big difference; if the statistical significance is calculated, the p value is found to be less than 0.05. That is, statistically speaking, this result would have occurred less than 1 time out of 20 (5%) by pure chance. This research finding is therefore publishable.

But suppose the numbers were just slightly different. Suppose that, of the group of 40 receiving the experimental drug, only 28 got better and 12 did not. This level of significance is less than 0.05, and the results are therefore not publishable. The researcher looks at this result and tries to convince himself or herself that there really is beneficial effect there. Fully 28 people got better with the drug, a number far higher than 20 people who got better on their own, and there may not be time or funds to continue the experiment to obtain statistical significance. So the researcher looks at the experiment again to see if there is something to be salvaged. Suppose he or she finds that one of the patients in the 40 who received the drug was not totally honest in reporting his or her case history. Suppose the researcher concludes that this person should not have been in the 40 test cases in the first place, and therefore drops this person from the calculations. Now there are 39 subjects who receive the drug, and 28 are cured while only 11 still have the disease. This again is statistically significant and publishable.

Is such data manipulation unethical? Yes, if the researcher does not report what was done. If the paper reports that the study started out with 40 participants receiving the drug but that one patient was found to be ineligible, then this is aboveboard and scientifically honest. Unethical conduct would then occur when the researcher fails to mention how the calculations were done.[4]

Not only does this arbitrary limit present a temptation to cook the data, but the setting of this number is a foolish kowtowing to the statisticians. If the disease is an important one and if your new medicine clearly is helping people prevent it, then why can't the study be published, reporting, say, a 0.06 level of significance? The reader is warned that it is not less than 0.05, but the intelligence of readers is acknowledged by allowing them to make the decision whether to believe the data or not. To choose some arbitrary level such as 1 in 20 just leaves the researcher in a vulnerable position and prevents the publication of information that might be of value to some readers.

While the problems of statistical interpretation and data manipulation do not often exist in the humanities, fraud can still occur and be discovered. Historians, for example, use documents to produce evidence that challenges other interpretations, and the origin and validity of these documents must be truthfully stated. Forged documents, spurious fossils, or imaginary interviews have all been published in the scholarly literature. The withholding of information, while not strictly fraud, can certainly be considered uncollegial and bad form. Publication of the Dead Sea Scrolls is a prime example of how some select archaeologists have been able to milk the information for years without sharing it with others.

In the humanities, the greatest single sin is plagiarism—the theft of intellectual property. In one notorious case of apparent theft of intellectual property, substantial portions of the published work by a world-renowned historian from the University of Maryland were found to resemble another preexisting work. On the face of it, there seems no doubt that he stole some passages, but he denied that he purposefully copied the material. He claimed that much of the material in question might have stuck in his head from reading many books, and he wrote it down without consciously plagiarizing it.

This is possible, of course. Why would someone of his stature and eminence endanger his academic standing by plagiarizing the works of others? He does not need another book or paper to further his career, so his motive is not clear. Perhaps he was simply careless and sloppy, using phrases and ideas that he assimilated from others without properly attributing them.

For experienced professors, this is an understandable and sympathetic argument. We all have added material to our class notes, inserting interesting arguments, insights, and conclusions without the necessary care in attribution. A lecture, after all, is not meant to be an original presentation, but a compilation and synthesis of the state of knowledge in a given topic. Sometimes the ideas or words we use in a lecture are so good and fit us so comfortably that we begin to forget where they came from. They begin to belong to us, and we pretend subconsciously that we made them up. A particularly clever turn of phrase, a humorous aside, or an insightful conclusion—material for excellent lectures—all may have been purloined from others. We are often in a hurry and do not always take care to write down the source of good stuff we use in a classroom.

The professor runs little risk of plagiarism as long as the material stays oral and within a classroom. But many of us (this author included) make a habit of turning our courses into books. I have been teaching for more than 30 years. Which of the ideas in *this* book are truly mine, and which have I borrowed from others? I want to believe that I have carefully and conscientiously attributed others' intellectual property, but in all honesty I cannot confirm that. So how much of this book is plagiarized? I don't know, and I hope none of it is. But if a reader perchance recognizes any work belonging to others, I would be only too glad to attribute this in future editions.

In the end, candor and honesty and thoroughness are valued and absolutely essential in academics, whether in the sciences or in the humanities. The need for truthfulness in the reporting and publishing of scholarly information is easy to understand if we consider the alternative. Nothing in literature would be believable. All research projects would have to begin from basic principles and primary sources. The publication of truthful research and scholarship would eventually cease, and the game would be destroyed.

Joseph Bronowski, an eminent scientist, summed it up like this:

> All this knowledge, all our knowledge, has been built up communally; there would be no astrophysics, there would be no history, there would not even be language, if man were a solitary animal. What follows? It follows that we must be able to rely on other people; we must be able to trust their work. That is, it follows that there is a principle which binds society together, because without it the individual would be helpless to tell the truth from the false. This principle is truthfulness.[5]

Conflict of Interest

When the university or college pays you your annual salary, it expects you to work for this salary. As with other salaried people, you the professor are never "off duty." Professors are "on the job" all the time.

The exception to this rule involves private consulting. Universities condone and even encourage consulting at usually no more than one day per week. They justify this by assuming that the work you do outside the university will be valuable experience that you will bring to the classroom. Your consulting should therefore be in fields that you teach at the university. If a mechanical engineer becomes an expert on wine tasting and spends one day per week as a highly paid consultant for a vintner, this is not consulting that the university would consider beneficial to his or her job or the university. Thus, consulting in areas other than your professional expertise would be morally wrong.

But this idea turns on its head when the professor decides to establish or becomes managerially involved in a company that sells services or products in the area of his or her professional expertise. The university must wonder how such commitments can avoid interfering with professorial duties at the university. Even more problematical is the case where the company does business with the university, even though this business might be conducted indirectly through several companies. For example, a computer software company owned by a professor might sell its products to IBM, but IBM might then sell the PCs (with the software installed) to the university. This appears to be a clear conflict of interest.

Universities have all adopted policies governing conflicts of interest. Stanford's conflict of interest statement is typical:

> A conflict of interest occurs when there is a divergence between an individual's private interests and his or her professional obligations to the university such that an independent observer might reasonably question where the individual's professional actions and decisions are determined by considerations of personal gain, financial or otherwise.[6]

The federal government, which finances most research, has also been trying to figure out how to set rules for conflicts of interest. One attempt to write such rules was in 1989, and in this policy the university researcher was barred from owning stock in companies that might ultimately benefit from the research—an impossible requirement. Eventually the National Institutes of Health decided to allow each university to establish its own guidelines. Typical university guidelines require scientists to disclose payments of any kind from companies related to their research, and conflict is questioned only if these payments are more than $10,000 or amount to more than 5% of the value of the enterprise.

Conflict of interest does not always have to be financial, of course. Every researcher's theories or models are always being evaluated against other theories or models, and great satisfaction can come from the recognition that the entire field has found your pet theory to be the best explanation of nature, or has found your written material to be worthy of assigning as reading to students. Protection of such property can also cause conflicts of interest.

Professors have sometimes established private firms, using the knowledge and experience they have gained doing research at the university. Some of these firms, such as Hewlett-Packard, have been immensely successful. Because the university has little control on faculty time, and because such firms can provide potential income to the university, the trend has been to allow faculty to do whatever they want to as long as the prestige generated is high to the university. The greater the prestige attained by the professor and/or the company, the less likely the university is to interfere.

But there is something unseemly when large profits are realized by professors who have started their own companies while employed by a university. The university is not a profit-making venture and should not be used as a means of creating personal profit for its members. Even though Americans admire entrepreneurial skills, there is a limit to what professors are expected to earn from such activity. If they get so rich (think the faculty), then they must have not put in their fair share of the teaching or civic activity and this must have been a conflict of interest. Obviously this may be an unfair criticism, but the gaining of great wealth (by professorial standards) by faculty entrepreneurs is socially frowned on.

Finally, a potential conflict of interest can occur if you are asked to act as a tutor for a student in your course. You should decline, of course, and refer the student to the tutoring service of the university, or suggest graduate students who might be willing and able to help. But under no circumstances should you or the graduate student associated with the course accept money from the student for tutoring. If students not in your own course ask for help, you should refer them to their instructor. The only tutoring you can ethically do is for students not enrolled in your university or college.

Copyrights and Patents

By historical convention, the copyrights of all books written by faculty on university time, and the income derived from these books (royalties), belong to the individual professor. The university does not share in such income, arguing that the salaries of faculty are low in comparison to other fields and that this is a nice perk to have.

Although I have been the beneficiary of such royalty income, I always find myself being mildly embarrassed in keeping the money. I have used the university computers, I have used their library resources, I have used their photocopy machines, and I have written the books while fully employed by the university. Should the university not share in the income?

It would be quite difficult for any one university to change the royalty policy, however, since it would find itself severely at a disadvantage in hiring faculty, especially productive faculty, and so the system will remain.

Patents are another story. Most universities have established patent policies that in essence share the income derived from the licensing of patents. If you have invented something, say a new insect repellent, and you did this while working in the university laboratories, you fall under the university patent policy. The patent you obtain will be in your name, but the income will be split according to some formula, usually 50-50. This agreement gives the university an incentive to market your patents, and many universities have aggressive marketing strategies for their patents, especially in the medical center and in the life sciences.

The sharing of patent-derived income with the university can lead to ethical lapses, especially if the income potential is great. At Duke University some years ago, a researcher in the medical center invented a new device that he believed would have great potential for income, and instead of patenting it through the university, he claimed that his 16-year-old son had invented it independently, an unlikely event and a seemingly clear violation of ethical standards.

Moral Responsibility to and of the Professorate

In the old movie *Teachers,* the principal of the high school stayed hidden in his office and did not want to know what was going on in the high school. When he was called before the school board and asked about a serious incident, he could honestly say, "I don't know about that."

The ignorance of wrongdoing that goes on around us is lamentable but not indictable, and professors are notorious for keeping their distance and not nosing into the actions of their colleagues. There is nothing to be gained, they argue to themselves, by interfering in the affairs of colleagues, even if the actions are so egregious as to make them blush with shame.

Consider the faculty member who received a training grant from a governmental agency. She was responsible for recruiting and advising graduate students who would receive a master's degree on graduation. Because she was in total control of the funds, with no oversight by the departmental chair or other administrator, she decided to have the students take independent study summer courses under her direction. With 10 students signed up and paying summer school tuition (the money coming from the training grant), she then got paid for a month of summer salary. But the course was a sham. The students did not go to class, and some even traveled overseas for the summer. Regardless, at the end of the summer term, they all got three graduate course credits. One could argue that such a scam is close to fraud—awarding credit for no work so that the professor can receive the summer salary supplement. But even if the rest of the members of the department learn about the scam (through the grapevine), there is little chance that the guilty professor would suffer consequences. Nobody would blow the whistle because the effect would be to harm themselves as members of this department. Better to keep such knowledge to themselves and ignore the problem, they would argue. Like the reclusive high school principal, they can always say, "I did not know."

Michael Lewis distinguishes between "ordinary wrongdoing" and sins of many academicians. In his view ordinary wrongdoing is when one breaks the law, like getting a traffic ticket. But academic wrongdoing is not ordinary because it

> represents a grievous departure from those moral and ethical precepts that are to the academy's justifying purpose what the tree's limbs are to the trunk. Truth cannot be served dishonestly; to do so is a contradiction in terms. If it is to be served, it cannot be held hostage to the pursuit of personal gain and advantage. It cannot tolerate incompetence. And it cannot be left to the languid mercies of the lazy and the irresolute.[7]

Notes

1. Bok, S. (1978). *Lying: Moral choice in public and private life.* New York: Pantheon.
2. McCabe, D. (1992, Fall). The influence of situational ethics on cheating among college students. *Sociological Inquiry, 63*(3).

3. In my younger days I taught a large environmental pollution class for all comers. I assigned a term paper with open topics as part of the course. When I saw the same term paper for the third time I realized I had a problem, but I could not accuse the "writer" because I had not kept the two previous copies. We did, however, have a serious heart-to-heart talk, and I did scare the bugeebies out of him. Maybe that was for the best.

4. This example is on the videotape *Do Scientists Cheat?*, a NOVA program produced by the Public Broadcasting System.

5. Quoted by Ian Jackson. (1894). *Honor in science* (p. 7). Sigma Xi, from J. Bronowski, (1956). *Science and human values* (p. 73). New York: Messner.

6. Kennedy, D. (1997). *Academic duty* (p. 250). Cambridge, MA: Harvard University Press.

7. Lewis, M. (1997). *Poisoning the ivy* (p. 10). Armonk, NY: M. E. Sharpe.

CHAPTER 13

Getting
Fired

The Bath Iron Works, Maine's largest employer, is one of only two American shipyards capable of building naval vessels.[1] The executives of Bath Iron Works (BIW) were meeting with Navy personnel over the bidding process for the construction of five new destroyers. The executives were nervous. BIW needed this contract to stay in business.

At the conclusion of the meeting, a Navy consultant inadvertently left behind a confidential report that outlined the bidding procedures of the Bath Iron Works and its competitor. This document contained all the numbers BIW needed to prepare a successful proposal, because it was now able to predict how its competitor would structure its bid.

The document reached the desk of William Haggett, BIW's chief executive officer, who immediately realized the value of the document but also recognized the danger of such forbidden information. He knew that when bidding on government contracts, the contractors must sign a statement certifying that they have not used proprietary information in the preparation of their bid documents. He figured that they could use the numbers, then return the original document to the conference center, shred all of the hard copies, and if the issue ever came up, be able to say in all honesty that "no copies exist."

CEO Haggett was in a hurry to leave for a meeting in Portland and, on his way out the door, ordered the document copied and distributed to the estimators. While he was gone. the numbers were churned into the spreadsheets in preparation for the final bid.

Some members of the BIW executive group, however, were very uneasy about what they were doing and asked for advice from the company president. After considering the issue the president ordered all copies of the report shredded, the numbers expunged from the spread-sheets, and the original document delivered to the Navy officials.

After an internal investigation and an inquiry by the Navy, BIW was cleared of major wrongdoing, and the bidding process was allowed to continue. A few months later, William Haggett resigned. At a press conference, he admitted to having made a "bad decision." The 15 minutes of ethical uncertainty cost him his career. It was, in his words, a "career-ending move."

While many professors believe academia to be the safest, most secure of employments, professors are as susceptible to the dangers of career-ending moves as their business counterparts. In this chapter, I describe the actions that can result in career-ending moves and why academe uses such rules for the expulsion of its members.

Six Ways to Lose a Tenured Academic Job

Most university faculty handbooks or regulations spell out the means by which tenured professors can be fired. In most cases, these fall into six categories:

1. Dissolution of the department or program
2. Financial exigency
3. Gross incompetence
4. Willful neglect of duty
5. Moral turpitude
6. Professional misconduct

The first two reasons a university can remove a tenured professor are out of the control of the professor. Even the American Association of University Professors (AAUP), the watchdog of university adminis-trative propriety, recognizes that when a university decides to eliminate departments or programs, or when the very survival of the university is at stake, they can revoke tenure. While most universities make every attempt to reassign faculty to other departments, often this is impractical. Should a dissolution of a department occur, as it recently did when James

Madison University eliminated its major in physics, costing 10 faculty jobs, there is little individual faculty members can do to save their jobs.[2]

The last four reasons a university can fire a tenured faculty member are at least to some degree within the control of the professor.

Gross Incompetence. Several decades ago when faculty salaries were low, teaching positions plentiful, and faculty credentials minimal, some incompetent people got through the system and won tenure. Today, however, our rigorous system of recruitment and tenure rarely produces grossly incompetent faculty.

There is ethical backing for the use of gross incompetence as a cause for dismissal. If the professor is unable to perform a function for which he or she is compensated and which is expected of the professor by the students, the professor is misrepresenting himself or herself. Students expect at a minimum that professors be competent in their scholarly disciplines, and a breach of this agreement is clearly unethical.

Willful Neglect of Duty. Willful neglect of duty is clearly under the control of the individual. This career-ending move occurs because a professor shirks teaching duties. If professors simply meet their classes and give exams, they seldom face accusations of willful neglect of duty. Thus, research, advising, publishing, committee work, and all the other duties of a faculty member are secondary as long as the classes are met and some effort is made to teach the material. Professors have great latitude in how they teach, and it is difficult to remove a teacher for bad teaching. However, in at least one case, a professor was dismissed for neglect of duty for losing control of classes and making the exams so difficult that no students were able to pass them.[3]

The ethical reasons for dismissal due to a willful neglect of duty are fairly obvious. Not performing one's function is simply receiving compensation for services not rendered. Where this situation can become interesting, however, is when the teaching professor does not teach what he or she is assigned to teach. For example, a physics professor might teach an introductory physics course as a course in metaphysical reasoning, or another instructor might teach it as an engineering course. Are these professors guilty of a neglect of duty?

I do not believe that in these cases the defense of academic freedom is persuasive. An unorthodox introductory physics course places students at a distinct disadvantage when they take higher-level physics, or engineering courses that presume a basic understanding of physics. It would seem to be in the best interests of the students and the university to require faculty to teach uniform introductory courses, and a failure to do so should be construed as a willful neglect of duty.

In the humanities, where knowledge does not necessarily occur in a linear fashion, the question of consistency is less clear. If the course is on creative writing, the readings chosen by the various professors would no doubt vary widely with no ill effect. Neglect of duty would occur if the professor of a creative writing course taught Oriental religions instead of creative writing. The expectation is that the course follows its catalog description, which is a contract between the students and the faculty. For the professor to not honor this contract is a willful neglect of duty.

Moral Turpitude. Moral turpitude in this context generally means either a serious crime or some form of sexual misconduct. Most charges having to do with sexual misconduct never become public. If the charge is serious, the professor is often given the opportunity to resign, sparing his or her family the ordeal of a public hearing and formal dismissal. The problem with such a procedure is that the dismissed professor might find academic employment at a new school that would be unaware of the moral transgressions.

Occasionally professors charged with sexual misconduct choose to fight the charge, at which point all of the details become public. At the University of Kansas, a law professor was accused of sexual harassment and decided to face a faculty panel instead of quietly resigning. The panel found him guilty of moral turpitude, citing 18 violations of the code of conduct. He was dismissed.[4]

If the accused decides not to fight charges of moral impropriety, does the university have a moral obligation to make the offense public and thus prevent a recurrence of a similar transgression? If the incident is swept under the rug, the offending professor would suffer only in that he or she loses tenure and has to find other employment. Should a repetition occur at another university, that institution and its students would suffer. Yet, if the details of the incident are made public, the professor's friends and family would be harmed and the victim may have to be identified.

In my opinion, the best solution is a compromise. Universities should make the incident and the firing public but not describe details beyond "dismissal because of a personal matter." This would publicize the fact that an incident had occurred. and any other institution intending to hire the dismissed professor could ask the appropriate questions. In this way, the person who caused the unfortunate incident is the only one who suffers the consequences of his or her actions. It is also then up to that individual whether or not to make the details public.

Definitions of sexual misconduct are murky. One yardstick is to ask whether the behavior will compromise the professor's duty. A romantic relationship with an undergraduate student is always out of bounds and can be cause for dismissal. Similar relationships with graduate students are also problematic, although marginally more acceptable, because of graduate students' higher maturity level. Even relationships conducted in private are not ethically acceptable because the effect on the student and on the student-faculty relationship is still potentially destructive. Other lascivious behavior, such as the display of prurient pictures, unwanted touching, and suggestive remarks, may be excused on the first offense, but seldom on the second. A career-ending move would be to forget one's role as the professor and assume that academic freedom includes sexual freedom.

We in the professorate consider such actions unethical because the professor takes unfair advantage of students by requesting sexual favors, making suggestive remarks, or exposing the unwilling recipient to an uncomfortable environment (for example, by displaying pornographic pictures or telling crude jokes). Sexual misconduct is especially problematic when a sexual encounter occurs between a professor and a consenting undergraduate student. Such a liaison is unfair to other students. Although both parties can be considered consenting adults, the younger participant might in later years regret the relationship. While there may not be an immediate threat of emotional harm to the student, the possibility of future harm should be sufficient cause for professors to resist all liaisons with students. If this is paternalism, it is paternalism at its best.

At universities supported by religious organizations, morals are sometimes interpreted in a religious sense, that is, immorality is what is sinful as defined by a religious order. Such a morals charge can be used to dismiss an undesirable faculty employee who might contaminate the students' religious beliefs. In one case, the Catholic University of Puerto Rico fired a tenured professor because she divorced and remarried outside the church.[5] At Seton Hall, another Catholic university, a teaching priest was fired after he resigned from the priesthood.[6] The St. Meinrad School of Theology fired a tenured professor because she challenged the Vatican's ban on female priests, and at Nyack College in New York a tenured faculty member was fired because she attached a button to her briefcase on which appeared "Support Gay Rights."[7]

In such instances, the universities are ethically correct. Faculty are hired at such schools with certain understandings of proper conduct. Nyack College, for example, ensures academic freedom only if the faculty "remain within the accepted confessional basis of the institution." After voluntarily and knowingly accepting an appointment at a school that enforces religious rules, ignoring or flaunting such rules can often result in a career-ending move.

Misrepresenting oneself professionally can be cause for dismissal based on moral considerations. Benedict College in South Carolina fired a faculty member who did not include on his résumé previous employment at another university. As it turned out, he had an outstanding warrant for his arrest in the previous state. The dismissal was not for the arrest, but for misrepresenting his experience.[8] A medical researcher at the Oregon Health Sciences University recently had to resign after the school discovered that she had falsely claimed to have earned an M.D.[9]

Moral turpitude also encompasses the breaking of laws. While major felonies are sufficient cause for dismissal, even petty crimes may be career-ending moves. A small Southern college fired a full professor accused of shoplifting a pack of pipe cleaners. The college president wrote:

> The general knowledge of your misconduct and inditement [sic] for shoplifting will diminish your effectiveness at this institute of Christian higher education. Because of this situation, your contract to teach at Philander Smith College will not be renewed.

It turned out that the professor had been at odds with the administration for some time over the future of the college, and the administration found the incident a convenient way to get rid of a troublesome faculty member.[10]

At the University of North Carolina at Chapel Hill, a tenured law professor lost his job for pilfering small items from a drugstore. He acknowledged his problem with kleptomania, and argued that this had nothing to do with his effectiveness as a professor. The faculty agreed with him and recommended reinstatement. But the chancellor, for reasons that appear to be designed to curry favor with the state legislators, dismissed the professor.

The breaking of laws also includes the misuse of research funds. An assistant professor of biology at Tulane was fired after conviction for improperly using federal funds for personal travel expenses, books, camera equipment, and for hiring a relative as a research assistant.[11] A president of the Northeast Texas Community College tendered his resignation because of accusations that he had misappropriated and misused college funds to renovate his home, repair his car, and contribute to political campaigns.[12]

Another form of moral turpitude can be the use of offensive language or profanity. While there is free speech in theory, the professor does not have the right to say anything he or she wants in the classroom. The use of hurtful speech, especially racially oriented hurtful speech, can be a career-ending move.[13]

In summary, if a professor transgresses the moral code at an institution, he or she can expect retribution or even a truncated career. It is up to the individual professor to understand just what that code is and what actions can result in career-ending moves.

Professional Misconduct. The last type of career-ending move is professional misconduct such as plagiarism, scientific fraud, or other scholarly improprieties.

Plagiarism comes in many forms, ranging from the presentation of other people's ideas as one's own to the outright theft of complete papers. One way of strengthening one's résumé is to pirate papers from obscure journals and present them as one's own work, perhaps publishing them in another obscure journal, counting on the sheer volume of published papers to prevent discovery. At the University of Virginia, one postdoctoral researcher pirated at least a half dozen research papers and may have plagiarized more than 55 publications.[14] Another researcher, while at Santa Clara University, published on average one paper every 10 days by making up the data or simply copying other papers. No human being, no matter how talented, could maintain such productivity. Why he was not exposed earlier is still a mystery.[15]

Career-ending moves can also simmer in obscurity only to destroy a career many years later. In one case the theft of data from a proposal by a junior associate resulted in the resignation of the tenured professor. The professor, then at the Yale University Medical School, received a scientific paper for review from a professional journal and gave the paper to this post-doctoral associate to review. The post-doc wrote the review (recommending rejection) and gave it to the professor to sign. Some months later, the two published in the *American Journal of Medicine* a paper suspiciously similar to the paper originally reviewed by the post-doc. An investigation showed that the post-doc lifted significant parts of the original paper and then fudged his own data. He resigned from his position. The affair was kept quiet and the professor went on to become the chief physician at Columbia Presbyterian. Some time later, Columbia officials found out about the incident and asked him to resign because he had displayed "ethical insensitivity" by not investigating the episode more aggressively.[16] In another case, a former director of the National Institute of Mental Health, who was also a senior psychiatrist at Harvard University Medical School and the general director of the McLean Hospital in Belmont, Massachusetts, lost his career after the discovery of plagiarized papers during his early research years.[17]

In one unusual case, a researcher not only copied major sections of a paper but referenced the original paper and even sent a draft of the paper to the original author for his comment. The author, then a sociologist at the California State University at Long Beach, published the article in *Sociology of Sport* under the title "Putting on the Game Face: The Staging of Emotions in Professional Hockey." His article referred to the earlier article titled "The Staging of Emotion: A Dramaturgical Analysis," which described the emotional preparation of football players. The hockey author clearly stated his intention to parallel the football article, but his imitation went too far. A page-by-page comparison of the articles shows that he lifted entire passages from the first article. When confronted with this evidence, the sociologist acknowledged that he had copied the material, but argued that he did so on purpose. It apparently never occurred to him that this constituted plagiarism.[18]

When the allegations came to light, he left Long Beach State voluntarily but under pressure, moving to a similar position at Valparaiso

University. None of the letters of reference received by Valparaiso University alluded to the plagiarism incident, and Valparaiso officials did not find out about it until the guilty sociologist published an official apology. Because of his lack of candor, Valparaiso decided not to renew his appointment.

Using even snippets of others' material is risky if one is a public figure. An interim president of the University of Minnesota borrowed some material and used it in a speech he gave on numerous occasions. When this plagiarism became public, he was forced to withdraw his name from consideration for the presidency of North Dakota State University. While this was not a career-ending move, it certainly derailed his attempts to obtain a promotion in academic administration.[19]

The basis for the immorality of professional misconduct lies in the admonition to be truthful. From this moral requirement follow all rules for professional conduct. One does not plagiarize because this is misrepresentation. One does not claim credit for work not done because this is untruthful. One does not steal ideas from research proposals because the subsequent publication of these ideas falsely implies that they belong to the author.

Justification for Moral Rules in Academia

Why does academia take these principles so seriously—seriously enough to expel one of its own when the principles are seriously compromised? I believe there are two reasons—one that represents the best of the professorate, and one that is considerably less attractive.

On the more favorable side, these rules of conduct (and sanctions for misconduct) are a part of academia because we recognize the immense responsibility we each play in the moral development of our students. While few professors discuss ethics and values in class, our students are keen observers of our value systems. If we support less than honorable conduct, students receive this message. If we conduct ourselves in a truthful, helpful, and caring manner, students discover these values in us as well (and perhaps in themselves).

Students remember and appreciate discussions of ethics. I once had a freshman student who, after doing poorly on a test, claimed that I was unfair for not giving him points because he *knew* the material. Even though his calculations were incorrect, he felt that I should not take off points for a wrong answer that showed knowledge of the course material. I shared this situation with the students in a junior-level class and we had a lively discussion on the merits of the case. After a thorough discussion the students agreed that his argument was not persuasive and that I should stick to my guns. After class one of the students came into my office and told me that, while he will certainly eventually forget the technical material we were slogging through in the class, he would always remember my bringing up the ethical problem for discussion.

Students have their ethical antennae up. If we fail them, they will be poorly served by higher education. I believe that most of us recognize this and, even if unconsciously, conduct ourselves ethically. And if we identify colleagues who do not have these values, we want to expunge them from the profession.

The second reason why we take these values so seriously is less benevolent. It seems to me that many of the rules developed by academia over hundreds of years are unique to this profession. These rules have helped foster the high standing academia enjoys within our society. The professorate has carved out a special place for itself, and there is no doubt that the academic life is highly attractive and sought after by many. (Witness the number of applications received during any faculty search.) Professors have the freedom to do what interests them, with very few restrictions and requirements. They teach what they like and undertake research in their area of specialization, all this with little accountability. Finally, they determine their own work schedule, and their workload is steadily decreasing. Although the numbers are sketchy, there is evidence that in higher education, the number of full-time students in the arts and sciences over the past decades has *decreased* while the full-time faculty in the arts and sciences has *increased*.[20]

Over the past 30 years, the time commitments of faculty in classrooms have steadily diminished, and the "best" universities reward productive faculty with decreased teaching loads. Faculty salaries have continued to increase, especially for the superstars at prestigious universities. In short, professors have it good, and they do not want anyone threatening this privileged position.

In order to maintain the status quo the professorate has developed guild rules on how to behave. Outside the military and the clergy, no profession has stricter guild rules and self-policing policies. Anyone caught breaking these rules is a threat to the culture and is either reprimanded or dismissed. Moral turpitude, for example, is especially sinful because parents entrust their children to the professors. If professors did not project an image of in loco parentis parents would not pay the exorbitant tuition they now do and professors' salaries and reputations would suffer.

Professors similarly value the rules of fair science and scholarship. The professorate recognizes that the institution of academia could not survive if it became commonplace to plagiarize and defraud. Academicians like the system as it is and the academic community makes every effort to police itself.

In summary, there are two reason why academicians adhere so closely to the guild rules. The first is the altruistic motive for the benefit of their students' moral development, and the second is the nourishment and survival of the culture that gives the professors so many benefits. Both of these are parts of what has evolved into a *good* system, and its support is ideally both a selfish and a selfless act.

Notes

1. The story is told by Rushworth Kidder (1994) in *How good people make tough choices.* New York: William Morrow.

2. *Chronicle of Higher Education.* (1995, May 26). *41*(37), p. A18.

3. Report. (1980, May/June). *Academe, 66*(3), p. 140.

4. *Chronicle of Higher Education.* (1995, May 26). *41*(37), p. A18.

5. Report. (1987, May/June). *Academe, 73,* p. 31.

6. Report. (1985, May/June). *Academe, 71,* p. 3.

7. Catholic seminary fires professor after statement on female priests (1995, May 26). *Chronicle of Higher Education, 41*(37), pp. A17, A18.

8. Report. (1994, May/June). *Academe, 80,* p. 3.

9. Office of Research Integrity. (1994, September). U.S. Public Health Service. *Newsletter, 2*(4).

10. Report. (1980, July/August). *Academe, 66*(4), p. 198.

11. In brief. (1987, October 27). *Chronicle of Higher Education, 33*(24), p. 2.

12. Misuse of college funds prompts offer to resign. (1995, March 13). *Chronicle of Higher Education, 41*(29), p. A8.

13. McMillen, L. (1986, December 17). Many colleges taking a new look at policies on sexual harassment. *Chronicle of Higher Education, 33*(16), p. 1. Gaiter, D. (1994, September 12). White teacher's use of a racial pejorative roils black campus. *Wall Street Journal, 227*(60), p. 1.

14. Roark, A. C. (1980, September 2). Scientists question profession's standards amid accusations of fraudulent research. *Chronicle of Higher Education, 27*, p. 5.

15. *Do Scientists Cheat?* NOVA, Public Television Video.

16. Roark, A. C. (1980, September 2). Scientists question profession's standards amid accusations of fraudulent research. *Chronicle of Higher Education, 27*(20), p. 5.

17. Noted Harvard psychiatrist resigns posts after faculty group find he plagiarized (1988, December 7). *Chronicle of Higher Education, 35*(15), p. A1.

18. Mooney, C. (1992, February 12). Plagiarism charges against a scholar can divide experts, perplex scholarly societies, and raise intractable questions. *Chronicle of Higher Education, 38*(23), p. A1.

19. Blum, D. (1988, July 27). Plagiarism in speeches by college presidents called "capital offense" and "ultimate sin." *Chronicle of Higher Education, 35*(11), p. A11.

20. Huber, R. (1992). *How professors play the cat guarding the cream.* Fairfax, VA: George Mason Press.

CHAPTER 14

The Academic Career

Thus far in this book, academic life is described as the life of the assistant professor. Obviously, many assistant professors become associates and then full professors, eventually retiring after glorious academic careers. In this chapter, I discuss how your career might develop and how, during this exciting ride, you are going to keep all the balls in the air.

Keeping the Balls in the Air

This is a true story: A State of Michigan lawmaker asked a professor at a public hearing how many hours he teaches. The professor answered honestly that he was teaching nine hours that semester. "Long day," said the senator. "Good thing it's light work."

Most nonprofessors have no idea how many hours we professors put in. They do not understand that "teaching" is a vague term that can cover anywhere from lecturing to 500 students to a quiet talk with a troubled student. They cannot understand why, on Sunday afternoons, we start to have anxiety attacks about how we can possibly keep all the balls in the air for another week.

Doing research, publishing papers and scholarly books, advising students, serving on committees, reviewing proposals for funding agencies, lecturing, correcting exams, reviewing articles for journals, serving on national panels, etc., etc. Aggggh!

The sources of stress among faculty was surveyed by the Higher Education Research Institute, with the summary of the results shown in Table 14.1.

The data show that the single most important source of stress is time pressure, and this is essentially constant regardless of the type of

TABLE 14.1 Sources of Faculty Stress, by Institutional Type and
Gender

	Percentage of Respondents Who Indicated the Source of Stress					
	All	All Men	All Women	Universities	Four-Year Colleges	Two-Year Colleges
Level of Stress in the Past 2 Years						
Extreme stress	34	29	46	35	34	33
Little stress	13	16	6	13	13	13
Sources of Stress						
Time pressure	85	81	92	85	84	84
Lack of personal time	81	76	91	80	81	81
Teaching load	68	64	75	62	70	72
Institutional "red tape"	68	69	68	69	68	67
Managing household responsibilities	66	61	76	63	65	73
Personal finances	61	59	63	59	61	62
Students	57	53	64	52	56	65
Colleagues	56	54	61	58	56	53
Committee work	54	52	60	54	54	55
Research or publishing demands	50	50	49	72	51	12
Subtle discrimination	26	20	39	26	28	23

SOURCE: Dey, E. L., Ramirez, C. E., Korn, W. S., & Astin, A. W. (1993). *The American college teacher.* Los Angeles: UCLA, Higher Education Research Institute.

institution. Women especially are concerned with the lack of personal
time. The other item that jumps out of the table is the high level of stress
among university faculty due to research or publishing demands.

More subtle sources of stress might come from the lack of reward
and recognition. Especially in teaching, nobody seems to appreciate what
I do. Another source of stress is the feeling of powerlessness—I know
what we ought to do to make this place rally great but nobody will listen
to me. Problems with professional identity creates tensions because your
compensation comes from the university but your academic standing is
determined by your peers at other institutions. Finally, there always are

problems with students—problems like seeing someone self-destruct and not knowing how to help.

Yes, being an active professor keeps you busy. But it is a good busy. You do mostly what you like. Even reviewing papers and proposals, often thought of as "altruistic work," gives you early insight as to what is happening in the field, an "early warning" that could prove very beneficial to your own work.

The trouble is, of course, that there is an infinite amount of stuff you could be doing at any one time. How are you going to juggle your time so as to maximize your efforts? Actually, the analogy with juggling is a good one,[1] and suggests a series of rules for time management.

Your job is to keep the balls in the air.

You cannot keep all the balls in the air simultaneously. There is only so much time and you have only so much energy. Some of the jobs that you think you should be doing simply will not get done.

You have some balls that are thrown at you, and you choose to throw others at yourself, even though this means dropping others. As a young faculty member you will be asked to share the burden of departmental administration, teaching the introductory courses that others no longer want to teach, and starting your research and academic studies. Having an enlightened departmental chair is a big help. The chair should not throw scud work at you during your probationary years. Jobs like advising the student chapter or arranging the departmental picnic can be done by others, and you should not be saddled with these duties.

You do not have to accept balls thrown by others. Avoid volunteering. Try to finesse committees that take a great deal of time, such as curriculum reviews. You have little to gain and a lot to lose.

You should seek advice from a more experienced person on which balls you can drop and which you should keep in the air. Try selecting an informal mentor. This senior person should have significant experience, a knowledge of the system, and a genuine willingness to help you plan your career. Take the time to get to know this person and seek advice on matters that affect your job.

You do not have to be perfect in choosing the right balls to drop. We all make mistakes. Seldom are such mistakes fatal to your career, as long as you keep trying and learning.

A more specific guide to time management has been proposed by Philip Wankat, consisting of practical rules to follow.[2] His list follows, with my embellishments:

- Set two 3-year goals. (For example, get two research grants, publish six papers.)
- Prioritize goals. ("Stay healthy" should be on top of the list.)
- List activities you need to do to achieve goals. (For example, write 10 proposals.)
- Prioritize activities. (A activities, most important; B, next; and C, not very. Make sure the A list stays short and is completed.)
- Work on A items when you are at peak efficiency.
- The A list should include smelling the roses.
- Set office hours and enforce them.
- Learn to throw people out of your office.
- Meet in the other person's office, not yours, so you can stop the meeting when appropriate.
- Schedule big blocks of uninterrupted time for the A list. Try to take one day a week to stay home. You do not have to make excuses when someone tries to schedule a meeting for that day. Just say, "I will not be in."
- Avoid perfectionism.
- Take breaks.
- Piggyback your work. Use the proposal as a professional paper and vice versa.
- Handle all snail-mail immediately, throwing most away. Do not allow mail to accumulate.
- Respond to all email in short (but friendly) messages.
- Learn how and when to say NO!

Another set of practical suggestions comes from a group of assistant professors, on the Internet (Tomorrow's Professor Listserv, reis@cdr. stanford.edu).[3] I am adapting their ideas, using my own words.

- Limit the number of different classes you teach each semester. Insist on teaching no more than two different courses.
- The time required to be a *great* teacher is many times that required to be a *good* teacher. Resist the temptation to be a great teacher even though you know you can be.
- Try to teach courses that other faculty are also teaching so you can use their stuff.
- Arrange your teaching schedule so that you have at least one free day a week. Do not schedule any meetings during that time. You will always have the excuse that you will be "off campus."
- Try to teach a graduate course and an undergraduate course in the same field. You will be surprised how one can feed off the other.
- Post frequently asked questions (FAQs) on your Web site.
- Try using "open office hours" when students can wander in and out of your office. You will find that help and explanations can be shared.
- Do not answer your telephone every time it rings. Especially do not answer it when there is someone in your office. A warm body always takes precedence over a ringing machine.
- Do not do consulting until after you have tenure. Consulting can be a huge time sink and will not help you at all in your quest for tenure.
- Volunteer for committees you want to be on. Then you can say "no" to other committees you do not want to be on.

In addition to juggling the balls that represent your work, you undoubtedly have other personal commitments. These decisions, such as going to the office on a beautiful Sunday afternoon when you could be taking the kids to the park or the soccer game, are the most difficult to make. There will be times when you begin to wonder what it would be like to work 8 to 5 and carry home an empty briefcase. I am sure, however, that when Thoreau talked about people who "lead lives of quiet desperation," he did not have professors in mind, but rather the guys with the empty briefcases.

Progression of Your Academic Career

As the years roll by and your career develops, you will go through various stages in your academic career. Table 14.2 is a useful summary of the various stages in your career.

The most important line in Table 14.2 is the last one, the hazards. Because you do not have to punch a time clock, and because you are so intensely involved in your work, there is a real danger of having your kids start calling you "Uncle Daddy" or "Aunt Mommy." You should recognize this hazard and consciously develop a plan for making sure that you do not neglect your family. I found that consciously and studiously not going to the office on weekends provided me with a lot of time with the family, even though I brought work home and spent many late Sunday nights getting ready for the week. That plan seemed to work well, but you should have your own way of not being totally consumed by your work.

More important for senior faculty are the last stages, becoming deadwood and the onset of cynicism. The antidote to the deadwood hazard is to continue to do research and scholarship. It is difficult or impossible to grow old when young minds are pushing you to learn new things. You have to stay current because once you let go of the skills that got you your Ph.D., it will be impossible to retrieve them, and you will indeed become deadwood.

There is another reason for doing research/scholarship. If for some reason you do not want to stay (or are able to stay) at the college where your started your career and will be out looking for a job, your chances of finding a position will be far better if you have continued to do research and scholarship. Even though many colleges today claim that they do not consider research or scholarship important in hiring, promotion, and retention, this is changing, with an increasing number of universities reporting that research is a major factor in granting tenure.[5]

The last item in the table is the most troubling. I have no cure for cynicism—except maybe to write a book on just how good this job really is.

TABLE 14.2 Faculty Career Stages

	Stage		
Novice Professor	*Early Academic Career*	*Mid Career*	*Late Career*

Theme

• Getting into the academic world	• Settling down and making a name	• Accepting a career plateau or setting new goals	• Leaving a legacy

Characteristics

• Growth • Feelings of intense pressure	• Mastery of principal faculty roles • Concrete goals • "Make-or-break" feeling	• Productivity • Questioning • Rewards • Feelings of plateauing	• Thoughts of retirement • Paradox: satisfaction with misgivings

Major Concerns and Activities

• Teaching competence • Starting a program of scholarship • Learning college culture, resources, policies, etc. • Juggling family and career responsibilities	• Refinement of teaching techniques • Notice as a scholar • Concern about future • Involvement in professional organizations • Service activity	• Desire for senior status in college • Worry about losing mastery • Heavy service activity responsibilities • Consideration of shift to administration	• Finishing significant projects • Pride in accomplishments • Concern about losing touch with discipline • Fear of isolation • Sense of being unappreciated

Hazards

• Neglecting family • Being consumed by teaching and neglecting scholarship	• Neglecting family • Vague anxiety • Overextension	• Becoming deadwood • Resenting younger faculty	• Cynicism • Isolation

SOURCE: Gibson, G. W. (1992). *Good start.* Bolton, MA: Anker (p. 227).

Epilogue[6]

One night a group of nomads were preparing to retire for the evening when suddenly they were surrounded by a great light. They knew they were in the presence of a celestial being. With great anticipation, they awaited a heavenly message of great importance that they knew must be especially for them.

Finally, the voice spoke. "Gather as many pebbles as you can. Put them in your saddle bags. Travel a day's journey and tomorrow night will find you glad and it will find you sad."

After the light departed, the nomads shared their disappointment and anger with each other. They had expected the revelation of a great universal truth that would enable them to create wealth, health, and purpose for the world. But instead they were given a menial task that made no sense to them at all. However, the memory of the brilliance of their visitor caused each one to pick up a few pebbles and deposit them in their saddle bags while voicing their displeasure.

They traveled a day's journey and that night while making camp, the reached into their saddle bags and discovered every pebble they had gathered had become a diamond. They were glad they had diamonds. They were sad they had not gathered more pebbles.

Looking back at a career in academia, it is the rare professor who would admit that he or she should not have gathered more pebbles along the way. Now *you* have a chance to fill your saddle bags. And I hope all your pebbles become diamonds.

Notes

1. The original idea is credited to Wanda Krassowska of the Department of Biomedical Engineering at Duke University.

2. Wankat, P. (1998, October). Efficiency for professors. In L. P. Grayson & J. M. Biedenbach (Eds.), *Proceedings of the 17th Annual Frontiers of Education Conference, ASEE,* pp. 207-211.

3. Kyle Catani (UNC), Wendell Gilland (UNC), Sunuil Kumar (Stanford) and Lisa Pruet (UC Berkeley).

4. Gibson, G. W. (1992). *Good start.* Bolton, MA: Anker, p. 227.

5. Seldin, P. (1989). How colleges evaluate faculty. *AAHE Bulletin,* 41.

6. Canfield, J., & Hansen, M. V. (1995). John Wayne Schlatter, quoted in *A second helping of chicken soup for the soul.* Deerfield Beach, FL: Health Communications.

Appendix

Supplementary Readings

The University and Academic Life

Anderson, M. (1992). *Impostors in the temple*. New York: Simon & Schuster.

Andrews, H. A. (1995). *Teachers can be fired!: The quest for quality*. Chicago: Catfeet Publishing.

Betcher, T. (1989). *Academic tribes and territories: Intellectual enquiry and the culture of disciplines*. Bristol, PA: Society for Research into Higher Education, Open University Press.

Bowen, H. R., & Schuster, J. H. (1986). *American professors: A national resource imperiled*. New York: Oxford University Press.

Boyer, E. L. (1987, 1994). *A classification of institutions of higher education*. Princeton, NJ: Carnegie Foundation for the Advancement of Teaching, Princeton University Press.

Boyer, E. L. (1990). *Scholarship reconsidered: Priorities of the professorate*. Princeton, NJ: Carnegie Foundation for the Advancement of Teaching, Princeton University Press.

Cahn, S. M. (1986). *Saints and scamps: Ethics in academia* (Rev. ed.). Landham, MD: Rowman & Littlefield.

Cornford, F. M. (1908). *Microcosmographia academica: Being a guide for the young academic politician*. London: Bowes & Bowes.

DeGeorge, R. T. (1997). *Academic freedom and tenure: Ethical issues*. Landham, MD: Rowman & Littlefield.

Hamilton, N. (1995). *Zealotry and academic freedom*. New Brunswick, NJ: Transaction Publishers.

Hoekema, D. A. (1994). *Campus rules and moral community*. Landham, MD: Rowman & Littlefield.

Huber, R. M. (1992). *How professors play the cat guarding the cream*. Fairfax, VA: George Mason University Press.

Kennedy, D. (1997). *Academic duty*. Cambridge, MA: Harvard University Press.

Kimball, R. (1990). *Tenured radicals: How politics has corrupted our higher education*. New York: Harper & Row.

Lewis, M. (1997). *Poisoning the ivy: The seven deadly sins and other vices of higher education in America*. Amonk, NY: M. E. Sharpe.

Markie, P. J. (1994). *A professor's duties: Ethical issues in college teaching.* Landham, MD: Rowman & Littlefield.

Palmer, P. J. (1983). *To know as we are known: A spirituality of education.* San Francisco: HarperCollins.

Rojstaczer, S. (1999). *Gone for good.* New York: Oxford.

Rosovsky, H. (1990). *The university: An owner's manual.* New York: Norton.

Sykes, C. (1988). *Profscam: Professors and the demise of higher education.* Washington, DC: Regency Gateway.

Community Colleges

Cohen, A., & Brewer, F. B. (1989). *The American community college.* San Francisco: Jossey-Bass.

Eaton, J. (1994). *Strengthening collegiate education in community colleges.* San Francisco: Jossey-Bass.

O'Banion, T. (1994). *Et al teaching and learning in the community college.* Washington, DC: American Association of Community Colleges.

Guides for the Job Search

Anthony, R., & Roe, G. (1984). *Finding a job in your field: A handbook for Ph.D.s and M.A.s.* Princeton, NJ: Peterson's Guides.

Fiebelman, P. J. (1993). *A Ph.D. is not enough: A guide to survival in science.* Reading, MA: Addison-Wesley.

Heiberger, M. M., & Vick, J. M. (1992). *The academic job search handbook.* Philadelphia: University of Pennsylvania Press.

Lewis, A. (1988). *The best résumés for scientists and engineers.* New York: John Wiley.

Showalter, E., Figler, H., Kletzer, L. G., Shuster, J. H., & Katz, S. R. (1996). *The MLA guide to the job search.* New York: Modern Language Association.

Academic Guidebooks for Young Faculty

Boice, R. (1992). *The new faculty member: Supporting and fostering professional development.* San Francisco: Jossey-Bass. [This is written to support the idea of faculty development, but it also has some good guidance on what is important for young faculty to know. The field is specifically psychology, but it is applicable to other disciplines as well.]

Davidson, C., & Ambrose, S. (1994). *The new professor's handbook: A guide to teaching and research in engineering and science.* Bolton, MA: Anker.

DeNeef, A. L., & Goodwin, C. D. (Eds.). (1995). *The academic's handbook* (2nd ed.). Durham, NC: Duke University Press. [Probably the best overall edited collection of essays for young faculty.]

Gibson, G. W., (1992). *Good start: A guidebook for new faculty in liberal arts colleges.* Bolton, MA: Anker. [An excellent book, well written and interesting. A must for the beginning liberal arts professor.]

Schoenfeld, A. C., & Magnan, R. (1992). *Mentor in a manual: Climbing the academic ladder to tenure*. Madison, WI: Magna Publications. [A thorough and practical guide to the young faculty member.]

Zanna, M. P., & Darley, J. M. (Eds.). (1987). *The complete academic: A practical guide for the beginning social scientist*. New York: Random House.

Teaching

Aleamoni, L. (Ed.). (1990). *Techniques for evaluating and improving instruction*. San Francisco: Jossey-Bass. [This book comes under the heading of "I wish I had written that." If you have to ever defend the use of student evaluations of teaching, this book is an absolute necessity.]

Boschman, E. (1987). *Ten teaching tools: Ten secrets to total teaching success*. Dubuque, IA: Kendall/Hunt.

Braskamp, L. A., Bandernburg, D. C., & Orly, J. C. (1984). *Evaluating teaching effectiveness: A practical guide*. Beverly Hills, CA: Sage.

Brookfield, S. D. (1987). *Developing critical thinkers*. San Francisco: Jossey-Bass.

Brookfield, S. D. (1990). *The skillful teacher: On technique, trust, and responsibleness in the classroom*. San Francisco: Jossey-Bass.

Brookfield, S. D. (1995). *Becoming a critically reflective teacher*. San Francisco: Jossey-Bass.

Diamond, R. M. (1989). *Designing and improving courses and curricula in higher education*.

Ebly, K. E. (1988). *The craft of teaching* (2nd ed.). San Francisco: Jossey-Bass. [This is a classic, full of good advice and personal experiences.]

Elbow, P. (1986). *Embracing contraries: Explorations in learning and teaching*. New York: Oxford University Press.

Ericksen, S. C. (1984). *The essence of good teaching*. San Francisco: Jossey-Bass.

Fuhrmann, B. S., & Grasha, A. F. (1983). *A practical handbook for college teachers*. Boston: Little Brown.

Kemp, J. E. (1985). *The instructional design process*. New York: Harper & Row.

Lambert, L. M., Tice, S. L., & Featherstone, P. H. (1996). *University teaching: A guide for graduate students*. New York: Syracuse University Press.

Lowman, J. (1984). *Mastering the techniques of teaching*. San Francisco: Jossey-Bass.

McKeachie, W. J. (1994). *Teaching tips* (9th ed.). Lexington, MA: D. C. Heath. [A classic; addressing many of the issues college teachers face in the classroom.]

Meyers, C. (1986). *Teaching students to think critically: A guide for faculty in all disciplines*. San Francisco: Jossey-Bass.

Ory, J. C., & Ryan, K. E. (1993). *Tips for improving testing and grading*. Newbury Park, CA: Sage.

Palmer, P. (1998). *The courage to teach: Exploring the inner landscape of a teacher's life*. San Francisco: Jossey-Bass.

Ramsden, P., (1992). *Learning to teach in higher education*. London: Routledge.

Tannen, D. (1990). *You just don't understand*. New York: Ballantine.

Wankat, P. C., & Oreovicz, F. C. (1993). *Teaching engineering*. New York: McGraw-Hill. [This book is a must for young engineering faculty.]

Writing Books and Scholarly Papers

Albrecht, W. S., & Gilaldi, J. (1985). *The MLS style manual.* New York: Modern Language Association. [The standard manual for language and literature, also periodically updated.]

American Psychological Association. (1994). *Publication manual of the American Psychological Association* (4th ed.). Washington, DC: Author. [The standard manual for all social sciences.]

Booth, V. (1985). *Communicating in science: Writing and speaking.* New York: Cambridge University Press.

Contore, J. A., & Gregory, J. M. (1993). *Engineering communications with confidence and reliability.* Dubuque, IA: Kendall/Hunt.

Haup, K. W., & Pearsall, T. E. (1984). *Reporting technical information* (5th ed.). New York: Macmillan.

Krull, L. (1989). *Twelve keys for writing books that sell.* Cincinnati, OH: Writer's Digest.

Levine, M. L. (1988). *Negotiating a book contract: A guide for authors, agents and lawyers.* New York: Moyer Bell.

Michaelson, H. B. (1990). *How to write and publish engineering papers and reports.* Phoenix, AZ: Oryx. [The best single work for publishing scientific and technical papers.]

Samuels, M. (1989). *The technical writing process.* New York: Oxford University Press.

Smith, J. G., & Vesilind, P. A. (1966). *Report writing for environmental engineers and scientists.* Woodsville, NH: Lakeshore Press.

Trelease, S. F. (1958). *How to write scientific and technical papers.* Baltimore, MD: Williams & Wilkins. [A classic: still useful after all these years.]

University of Chicago Press. (1982). *A manual of style.* Chicago: Author. [The standard manual for the humanities, periodically updated.]

Learning Theory

Block, J. H. (Ed.). (1971). *Mastery learning: Theory and practice.* New York: Holt, Rheinhart & Winston.

Fosnot, (Ed.). (1996). *Constuctivism: Theory, perspectives and practice.* New York: Columbia University, Teachers College Press. [This can be heavy going for the uninitiated. The chapter reviewing constuctivist learning theory is excellent and understandable, however.]

Gardner, H. (1985). *Frames of Mind: Theory of Multiple Intelligences.* New York: Basic Books.

Grayson, L. P., & Biedenbach, J. M. (1974). *Individualized instruction in engineering education.* Washington, DC: American Society for Engineering Education.

Johnson, D. W., & Johnson, R. T., (1989). *Active learning: Cooperation in the college classroom.* Edinal, MN: Interaction Book.

Steffe, L., & Gale, J. (Eds.). (1995). *Constuctivism in education.* Hillsdale, NJ: Lawrence Erlbaum.

Stice, J. E. (Ed.). (1987). *Developing critical thinking and problem solving abilities* (New directions for teaching and learning, No. 30). San Francisco: Jossey-Bass.

Gender Issues

Belenky, M. F., Clenchy, B. M., Goldberger, N. R., & Tarule, J. M. (1986). *Women's ways of knowing: The development of self, voice and mind.* New York: Basic Books.
Caplan, P. J. (1992). *Lifting a ton of feathers: A woman's guide to surviving in the academic world.* Ontario, Canada: University of Toronto Press.
Deats, S. M., & Lenker, L. T. (Ed.). (1996). *Gender and academe: Feminist pedagogy and politics.* Lanham, MD: Rowman & Littlefield.
Dziech, F. W., & Weiner, L. (1990). *The lecherous professor: Sexual harassment on campus* (2nd ed.). Urbana: University of Illinois Press.
Paludi, M. A. (Ed.). (1990). *Ivory power: Sexual harassment on campus.* Albany, NY: State University of New York Press.
Schuster, M. R., & Van Dyne, S. R. (1985). *Women's place in the academy: Transforming the liberal arts curriculum.* Totowa, NJ: Rowman & Attenheld.

Videos

Department of Civil and Environmental Engineering. (1995). *Academic integrity: A bridge to professional ethics.* Durham, NC: Duke University. [Four short vignettes on academic integrity designed to promote discussion among students. $50 postpaid.]
Department of Civil and Environmental Engineering. (1996). *A stampede of zebras.* Durham, NC: Duke University. [Dramatization of a play by Robert Martin involving ethical lapses in life science research. $95 postpaid.]

Index

About
the Author

P. AARNE VESILIND is Professor of Civil and Environmental Engineering at Duke University. He is currently involved in research on waste management, including processes for dewatering wastewater residues, management of municipal solid waste, treatment of industrial wastes, and environmental ethics in engineering. He serves on many technical and professional editorial boards and has written nine books on environmental engineering, solid waste management, and environmental ethics. His book *Introduction to Environmental Engineering* incorporates ethics into an undergraduate environmental engineering course. His most recent book is *Engineering, Ethics and the Environment,* coauthored with Alastair Gunn.

Professor Vesilind received his Ph.D. in environmental engineering from the University of North Carolina in 1968. Following a postdoctoral year with the Norwegian Institute for Water Research in Oslo, where he developed a laboratory test for estimating the performance of dewatering centrifuges, and a year as a research engineer with Bird Machine Company, he joined the Duke faculty in 1970 as an assistant professor. In 1976-77, he was a Fulbright Fellow at the University of Waikato, Hamilton, New Zealand, and in 1991-92, he was a National Science Foundation Fellow at Dartmouth College. He served as chair of the Duke Department of Civil and Environmental Engineering for 7 years and was elected by the School of Engineering faculty to chair the Engineering Faculty Council. He is a former trustee of the American Academy of Environmental Engineers and a past president of the Association of Environmental Engineering Professors.